Outside Time

My Friendship with Wilbur

Outside Time

My Friendship with Wilbur

STEPHEN RICH MERRIMAN

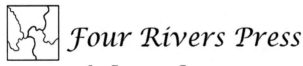 *Four Rivers Press*

SAN FRANCISCO, CALIFORNIA

BOSTON, MASSACHUSETTS

www.fourriverspress.com

Book design by Tim Kinnel, www.wordsareimages.com

Cover art by Joely Wilder Merriman. Used by permission of the artist.

ISBN 978-0-9817698-1-3

Library of Congress Control Number: 2008909168

Library of Congress subject headings:
1. Friendship. 2. Ice skating 3. Ice on rivers, lakes, etc.
4. Risk-taking (Psychology). 5. Death, Apparent.
6. After death communication 7. Spiritualism. 8. Consciousness.

To all those who feel called to heed
the lure to venture, literally or figuratively, out
upon river ice.

CONTENTS

ACKNOWLEDGEMENTS

The writing of a book, and its subsequent publishing, is always a nexus of creative, loving and supportive effort by a number of people.

In helping *Outside Time: My Friendship with Wilbur* find its way into the world, family, friends and professional helpers have contributed to the realization of this dream. I extend deep and abiding thanks to the following: first, my inveterate, cherished friend Wilbur Walworth, who taught me everything I know about river skating, and who had the courage, and curiosity, while he was dying, to enter into a very strange, post-death pact with his trusted friend; Wilbur's wife, Vivian Walworth, one of my staunchest and dearest friends over many years, who gave of herself generously in vetting the manuscript, and also supplied photos for use with the text; Emily Sara Taylor Merriman, my wife, loving critic and steadfast supporter, who was by my side that memorable April night in 2002 when the pact was honored; Joely Wilder Merriman, whose creative vision gave birth to the wonderful and moving painting that has become the cover image for *Outside Time*. Thanks also to H. D. Merriman and Hannah Bigelow Merriman for their review of, and sustained interest in, the manuscript and its contents; to Ann Davis Merriman and Edward Merriman, for their interest and shared comments on the text. It is with deep sadness that I note that neither Ann nor Ned lived long enough to see the book reach final publication; however, I am grateful that they each got to see the work in progress. Thanks also to Corinna Merriman-Morris, who braved the river—and Cape Breton—with me in earlier times. Special thanks to Bill Ryan and Jeanne Lightfoot, two of the most valuable readers any author could ever wish to have, for their loving and caring review of the text, and to old, noble friend Johnn O'Sullivan, for his fine professional discharging of copy editing responsibilities. I am also especially grateful to Tim Kinnel, whose superb design acumen and deft sense of craft created the overall look and feel of the book. The love and support of these wonderful people have made *Outside Time* possible. I am indebted to all of them.

Wilbur on the Sudbury—black ice!

Prologue

Life serves up certain experiences that carry with them the imperative to be shared. It may be that this is why these experiences happen at all: they have an impact on the experiencer—perhaps even an awakening, of sorts—and the news must be "put out there" in some fashion. These experiences may even be completable only to the extent that their being shared or made known is accomplished, or at least attempted.

So it was with my relationship with my dear friend Wilbur, a man I met on river ice in the late 1960s when I was in my early twenties and he was in his early fifties. That chance encounter led to a strange, wonderful and ultimately thrilling association that time wove on the loom of thirty-plus years. Chance encounter very, very gradually became friendship, and then, unexpectedly, kinship of a very special sort. This precious chapter of my life, now completed, left me with the sense that I was, to the best of my ability, meant to communicate about it.

This strange and wonderful connection, so randomly reinforced over the first twenty years or so, was, paradoxically, a kind of constant in my life as I traversed the territory from being a young man with certain fascinations (many of them destructive), on through young adulthood (including my first marriage and the rearing of young children), returning to school in my early thirties to embark on a new career, mid-life demolition (it used to be called "transition") in my late forties through early fifties, and restoration and renewal (in which I currently, gratefully abide).

For my friend Wilbur this span of years carried him over his own mini-epochs: late career culmination and "retirement," ongoing pursuit of naturalist interests and travels with his wife Vivian, devotion to inmate advocacy and the prisoner-run newspaper at the local penitentiary, outdoor adventures of all sorts, and then senescence and rapid, advanced decline.

I would like to think that out of the apparent randomness in which our friendship was birthed, each of us had a precious, unforeseen role to fulfill in the life of the other. In hindsight I recognize that our respective roles, over the years, passed back and forth, depending on context. Although, for most of our shared journey, neither of us would have thought of our presence in the other's life in terms of assuming, or living out, a "role," we each, nonetheless, completed what, for the most part, we didn't even know we were engaged in. As arcane as this sounds, it will all become clear with a reading of the narrative and its attendant commentary.

In more recent years I have come to recognize that God has blessed me with certain abilities as a writer, although I don't want to make too much of this. Actually, my fear, throughout the writing of this book, has been that whatever expressive gifts I may possess would fall short of what the account warrants — of what it deserves on its own merits. I have been somewhat comforted, and my reservations somewhat assuaged, by the recognition that the story itself, in its factual elements, is likely compelling enough to pull the reader along, notwithstanding whatever gaps and lapses exist in the rendering of it into language. I hope this proves to be so.

It was a privilege to know Wilbur, and it is a privilege to provide this account of one facet of his life — that involving our relationship with each other.

I hope that you, my readers, may be buoyed and uplifted by the account that follows. A "commentary and analysis" is included to help orient you as to the methodology and biases I bring to the recounting and reporting of it.

Yours, with the love of a kindred spirit,
Stephen Rich Merriman

August 15th, 2004
Chéticamp Beach, Cape Breton Island
Nova Scotia
Canada

Part I
The Narrative

*Winter on the Sudbury River, Concord, Massachusetts.
Black ice continues to thicken in the blistering, windswept
cold of a late January afternoon.*

WINTER

I

I don't recall the actual year, in the late 1960s, of that first winter when I ventured forth, solo, from the manicured ice of a cultivated urban pond (a seasonal overlay to summer tennis-court clay) out onto the wilder reaches of untamed river ice.

River ice is fashioned and worked by nature alone. It runs the gamut from crystalline, transparent black—on which one flies on an invisible membrane, and what meets the eye is the immensity of the inverted spatial canopy (water-filled) beneath, with only vertical fault lines, spread like lightning bolts, bearing evidence of a thickness capable of supporting whirling blades and a body—to porous, a deceptively safe-looking ice formed of one or more cycles of hard freeze, snow, thaw and refreeze—*looking safe*—an often multilayered ice/snow sandwich seducing through the appearance of a surface of solidness—but capable of being oh, so treacherous.

Pond ice certainly can be deadly also, for even in a hard freeze "warm" springs from underneath can thin a layer of ice, especially older ice, and one can unwittingly have ventured upon it without prior notice. But river ice is potentially much the more dangerous, for there are just so many ways it can fail you.

To begin with, the existence of ice on any pond or river, especially in temperate climes, is a bit of a miracle. Skatable ice even more so. A river that yields such a magical surface has to exist on the edge of weather that is cold enough to create it, yet not so cold as to close it out due to frequent snowfall. By these persnickety requirements, Eastern Massachusetts is about as good as it gets. The winters are generally cold enough to produce an ice blanket, while the proximity to the coast makes it likely enough that a fair percentage of winter storms will still come through as rain or sleet, rather than snow, thereby keeping skating alive. To live fifty or more miles to the north or west, say, in Southern New Hampshire, Southern Vermont or the uplands of Central and Western Massachusetts, the ice would, it's true, be quite a bit thicker, but it would be underlying frequent heavy snowfall, so good skating there would be very rare, indeed, and very short-lived. To live fifty or more miles further south, say, in Rhode Island or Eastern Connecticut, the hard freeze necessary to put down a base of black ice becomes considerably rarer, as well. It's true that snowstorms occur less frequently than to the north or west (good), but the ice itself is likely to be less thick and hard (bad).

In terming Eastern Massachusetts an "optimal" ice region for river skating, however, this should not be construed to mean that conditions suitable for river skating occur frequently. Such conditions are always rare. It *is* to say, however, that given the likelihood for such conditions to exist at all in any given winter, it is in Eastern Massachusetts that one is more likely to encounter them.

Yet, even in the optimal ice region of Eastern Massachusetts, ice has many enemies. The convincing hard-set of a cold snap may make the formation of ice on a watery surface (black ice, under these circumstances) seem unstoppable and irreversible, but the forces that would disband it are never not at work. Thaw in the form of warm air from above is one culprit—but only one. Geothermal heating (from below) is also ever in play, planing away at the undersurface, cavitating thickness into unevenness. River currents, as well, as in the increased velocity of water along the longer bank of a curve—the outside of a bend—and the changing velocity of water-flow between river narrowings and widenings—these all set up games of Russian roulette regarding where (and whether) it is safe to venture and where (or whether) not. Current-driven water freezes more slowly; ice is always thinner there. The interplay of wind and water—and the effects of the wavelets of a wind-whipped surface, ditto.

Then there are the freak freezes as in, for instance, a river rising to flood stage due to lots of rainfall, followed by a hard freeze (black ice everywhere) seizing marshes and low woodlands, and then, in the absence of further precipitation, the underlying water receding, leaving a layer of ice between the trees, clasping, and supported by, only their trunks—the ice otherwise undergirded solely by air and, many inches or more below, the receding water level. To skate on this ice is to skate on nature's hollow belly, as punctuated, if unlucky, by the concussion of collapsing ice unsupported by water, and immediate immersion into a frigid shallow bath.

On a river, no two freezes are ever the same. With each one, one has to "read" ice anew before ever skating a stride upon it. Otherwise, there are just too many ways for a river to get you.

II

So it was, that in a state of ignorance-born bliss combined with remarkable foolhardiness, I ventured forth onto the Sudbury River between Lincoln and Concord, Massachusetts one winter's day in the late 1960s. But I'll back up briefly. As I have said, I had been a skater primarily of outdoor ice since age five. Perhaps as a foreshadowing of events far in the future, that very first encounter with skatable ice had actually transpired on a river. My father, on one of our rare family outings, took my mother, my two brothers and me out onto the Muddy River, in summer months a stagnant, stinking, swamp that forms the connecting chain of Frederick Law Olmsted's "Emerald Necklace" along Boston's Fenway, transformed, in winter (weather permitting), into a series of skatable pond-links cut off by bridges. That first outing is still clear to memory. I was on lousy, dull-bladed skates (although at the time I couldn't know how handicapped I was due to this fact), and I did nothing but fall and bruise myself for about two hours. I must have spilled over a hundred times. The ice was soooooo slippery. It was pure misery. However, I was aware of other, much older skaters out there who could really move and cavort on the ice (some of whom were playing ice hockey). I was amazed at how they could get around. "I'll never be able to do that," I thought.

With the single exception of one other river outing hosted by a friend's family when I was about eight (in which we skated on frozen marshland that I was, as an unexpected coincidence many years later, to rediscover on my own), for the duration of my formative years my brothers and I belonged to a skating club that, as I have mentioned, flooded over tennis court clay to create about an acre's worth of shallow water pond. Inside the clubhouse, a serif-scripted maxim, ornately carved into a beam supporting a walkway above the oversized hearth, declared: "Power Perfected Becomes Grace."

For the following dozen years or so my winter life, social as well as athletic, revolved almost entirely around this club, and I became a truly devoted, excellent skater with lots of power, stamina, maybe grace, and certainly creativity. I used hockey skates, but could do the figure skate waltz jump on them, as well as "shoot-the-duck" (both forwards *and* backwards) along with various spread-eagle maneuvers on both inside and outside edges. On one occasion the Olympic champion Tenley Albright was practicing at the club. Mimicking her moves (while, of course, on hockey skates) I got a bit carried away. Aping more an unguided missile rather than a world-class figure skating champion, I miscalculated my trajectory—and hers—during this attempt to showboat, and managed to shoot-the-duck right into her. (She didn't see me coming at her under the radar.) Poor Tenley was brought down. On impact, she folded up like a wounded bat and came splat to the ice. I blushed with shame, sheepishness and embarrassment. She was not amused. I think I was about nine years old at the time.

On another occasion, when I was about thirteen, I decided, with a skating club friend, to skate one hundred laps of the pond at a good clip. This took quite a while to do. At the end of the ninety-ninth lap I impulsively chose, as a gesture of "good luck" en route to doing the final lap, to touch the railing of the wooden ramp leading down to the ice from the clubhouse. As I touched the railing, without slowing down, my balance was thrown off, and I lost it. I hurtled into the stanchion, bashing my forehead against it before flopping, stunned, to the ice, in a pool of blood. (My friend completed the hundredth lap—had he been the one to spill, I likely would have done the same.) A lump the size of a golf ball instantly mounded up on my brow. I was assisted into the clubhouse and a cold chisel was applied to my forehead to keep the swelling at bay. To this day, I still retain some extra subcutaneous girth from that memorable wipe-out.

However, these miscues and acts of delinquency notwith-standing, for several years running, as I got into my teens, I would win the annual club competitions for skating fast, in both the "forwards" and "backwards" events. On ice, I was built to move. I took this ability as my one, unassailable claim to fame.

With the family membership at this club drying up by the time I was about seventeen, polite, manicured, artificial pond ice (the pond was artificial, not the ice) and its attendant skating and adolescent antics were behind me. But my love of skating, by now so long ingrained, drove me to begin to explore real ponds, and then, rivers. I was, as I have said, a truly excellent skater, but I knew nothing about ice.

III

As I stepped onto true, unmanicured river ice, solo, for the first time, I was taken by the beauty held in a river of ice. Expanse . . . . . expanse . . . . . expanse . . . . . a ribbon of expanse widening here, narrowing there, wending along through hills, fields and woodlands, the only sound the wind that would sometimes send successive, narrow bands of small-grained snow tumbling across the ice, and an occasional report of concussion bearing witness to interior, shifting, seismic movements throughout what, as simply viewed, seemed massive, frozen and still. The ice was alive! This revelation was exciting; my breath shortened with the adrenalin of startled alertness.

That day (unlike a handful of others over the years) I managed not to get wet, though in my then-state of ignorance I could have been far closer to taking a terminal bath than I knew. Whether it was actually during this first solo venture onto virginal river ice, or by the end of the second or the third, that I met my river companion-to-be, I don't recall. However, certainly within that first, small handful of ventures onto this environment—all of which probably occurred within a week of the original voyage (to be responsive to the dictates of river skating requires on-the-fly recalibration of one's conventional life and schedule around the availability of ice—"Ice waiteth for no man"—) I had encountered Wilbur.

The actual number of times I ventured onto that river prior to my first encounter with Wilbur is of less importance than the fact that prior to meeting him, I was on my own on the ice, and at the mercy of dumb luck. Here's an example: Left to my own devices (and a little knowledge on a river can be as dangerous as none), I would timidly inch forth from shore, pathetically armed, in the absence of hockey stick or rope, only with the skate-blade toe of my awkwardly extended leg, tapping at the ice, trying to gauge thickness by watching for a crack in the ice (seeing if it ribboned vertically enough to indicate thickness). Somewhere I had heard that "It takes an inch of ice to hold you"—without the saying's specifying what *kind* of ice this would have to be. My temerity, and my rather inefficient, and often inaccurate, method of toe tapping left no room for error (which was an error). On my own, without guidance, I was categorically at risk. What is, therefore, of prime importance is that I met Wilbur at all.

While not recalling the particular number of times I had been on the river when first I met Wilbur, I do recall the moment. Alone on the ice, and inching along the shoreline, I became aware of a curious sound emanating from out of view, on the far side of a bend to my right. It was an irregular washboard sound, the waves of which seemed to be conducted to me both through air, and the membrane of ice as damped by water below. It was a rapid, irregularly paced rt-t-t-t-t-t-t-t-t-t-t-t-t-t-t-t-t-t-t that was, given the different densities of the media (air, ice and water) through which the waves reaching my ears were being transducted at varying respective speeds, both high-pitched and hollow.

All this registered, after a bit of a startle, fairly quickly. The mystery behind it was momentarily solved when the figure of a white-haired man coasted rapidly into view. He was slightly stooped, with a rigidly held, almost defensive posture, hockey stick firmly clutched forming a diagonal across the body, a length of coiled rope over a shoulder. He had strikingly attractive features, including a head crested with a shocking mound of white tousled hair accompanied by a matching set of eyebrows—all immediately visible. He was coasting fast, and was followed quickly by a large Samoyed, a white, cumulous cloud kind of dog. This strange man was utterly intent on what he was doing, covering "ground" at quite a clip, and obviously very much at home on this medium. To all appearances, he was having one hell of a good time for himself, totally immersed in his element. I felt a wave of instant deference arise in me.

He spotted me (cowering along the bank) and, upon seeing me, skated right over to where I was and came to a brief stop, with the billowing-coated pooch sliding to a stop immediately following. "How's the river?" I asked. No other introduction of any kind seemed necessary, or called for. "Not too bad—got to watch the outside corner of the bend leading to Route 117 from the bay, and you've got to pick your way through here and there. All things considered, not too bad." And he was gone.

It probably hadn't occurred to him to ask me about *my* "take" on the ice, or my discoveries out there (up close along the bank!). I'm sure he realized that there was no information forthcoming from me regarding the conditions on that river that could possibly be of any use to him. He was not at all discourteous. I didn't know his name; he didn't know mine. The details of personal identity were irrelevant. We were two people who had met on ice, and he had stopped to give me a traveler's report, and then, just as quickly, he was gone. The exchange was really one-sided, yet there is a kinship, as I was to learn, among those who dare to venture onto river ice. Information that holds sway over matters of life and death needs to be imparted succinctly, not elaborately or dramatically. It needs to be efficiently conveyed, not housed in pleasantries or effusive emotion. This was my introduction to Wilbur, the river wizard.

IV

Voluntary relationships are built one of two ways. The first, more usual way is that two people meet one another, discover an affinity between them, and start to hang out together. This is a standard prelude to friendship as well as more intimate relationships. The second way is that two people encounter one another in an environment that is ephemeral, yet recurring. In this modality relationships are built very gradually, based on repeat encounters that are determined by external factors. The environment, whatever it may be, and the two individuals' commitment to it are the ingredients that determine (a) that repeated encounters will occur at all, and (b) that repeated encounters will be succinct in nature, not extended, and not frequent.

Another feature of this kind of association is that it is not predicated, at least at the outset, on there being "growth," by way of change and evolution, in the relationship, per se. Such relationships are not structured along the lines of deepening interpersonal growth and development, as commonly understood. Rather, it is in the continuing aspect of sameness, predictability and reliability that such relationships take root, and find their value.

Regarding Wilbur, I came to know that any time there was a hard freeze in Eastern Massachusetts sufficient to put black ice in play on the Sudbury River, more often than not I would run into him out there on the far reaches. Just the sight of him with rope, hockey stick and Samoyed conveyed the assurance: The River is doable.

And we developed a "by thy sight shall thou knowest him" relationship in which spring, summer and fall were inconsequential. The first encounter of the new ice season was a seamless extension of the last freeze of the prior winter. Nothing had intervened, meanwhile.

V

At first I just observed Wilbur. His knowledge of rivers and ice was so thorough and his carrying of that knowledge so unassuming that it just naturally followed that I would start to imitate him, showing up at river's edge with hockey stick and rope in hand. I had seen how he would test the ice with swift, muscular, pointed jousts of the butt end of the stick, and what manner of information could be garnered from the report of concussed ice.

Such a simple thing, yet so revealing! A hockey stick with a circumference of tape at the end of the shaft, continuously wrapped to create a band the width of the tape but extending out perhaps 1/4" to 3/8" from the shaft: this was typical preparation (in addition to taping the blade) for the use of a hockey stick for ice hockey. But on a river, if you fell through the ice and someone was around to give quick assistance, a taped shaft could provide a "grip"—a point of leverage that could make it possible to be pulled out of the water back onto ice. Life and death could hinge on whether a hockey stick had a taped shaft end.

Also, the correct way to use a hockey stick on a river (unless one was actually playing hockey) was altogether different. Only when skating on already proven ice would Wilbur hold it in the usual hockey-player manner—a kind of stooped, at-the-ready-to-receive-a-puck-pass stance. When seeking to test and "prove" ice, however, Wilbur would, as previously noted, invert the hockey stick, clasping it firmly with one hand just below the blade, and decisively pound the ice with the butt end of the stick.

And what manner of information could be gleaned from such pounding! First, there was the "texture" of the ice that would be reflected in the aural quality of "thunk" and the range of vibration conducted up the shaft of the hockey stick with each impact. Using this method, Wilbur would gauge qualities of hardness and thickness (two independent variables) by feel alone. Then there was the visual information. Each pounding was forceful enough, by intention, to break through ice that was only marginally safe due to lack of thickness or poor texture, and so on. If a "pound" broke through to water beneath, this finding was instantly conclusive: the ice was not safe. As strange as it might sound, the intent *was* to break through the ice if it was at all possible to do so. A good, hard thwack that almost bounced back at you from the ice surface with hardly any scoring of the ice beneath was the gold standard, but a number of quite different parameters could be ascertained even in the absence of the "bounce," and in the aggregate they could also "prove" ice as being safe.

For instance, in ice that was at all clear Wilbur could read the pattern of fracture that the concussion of the stick would generate in the ice. In other words, how the ice dissipated each impact, and how the dissipation was revealed through the fracture pattern extending down into the ice, were very revealing. For example, a fairly shallow, contained zone of fracture, almost in the form of an "egg cup," extending down from the point of impact on the ice surface, would be sufficient to "prove" ice that might be only a few inches thick. Concussive patterns that would extend, like a piece of ribbon lying on its edge, could, through its meanders, reveal the thickness of an ice layer with exactitude. Also, the sound—the timbre—of the concussion as it would propagate between the ice layer and the water beneath would imply the overall viability of the ice sheet in the immediate vicinity.

These little examples are what might be called micro-assays of ice. To truly get to know how to read river ice, however, one also had to acquire a macro-picture of the river itself—its overall "habits" and tendencies vis-à-vis how, in the aggregate, it would freeze and thaw, refreeze, etc. This macro knowledge could only be acquired over a number of successive seasons, each of which would yield a number of "freezing cycles" of various types. There were certain bends that were more likely than not to be problematic in the way that they would freeze (and thaw). There were patches that froze into black ice with some regularity even when adjacent sections that looked about the same (river oriented in same direction, etc.) would not. One particular section of river would yield black ice almost regardless of other variables (such as wind direction and velocity) while the freezing patterns of other sections of river seemed extremely prone to the influences of wind. Also, recurrent patterns of freeze could, to some extent, be calibrated to the water level (always varying) of the river at the time of freeze. Similar water levels, in a given river, would yield identifiable types of freeze.

Perhaps as important—in fact, certainly as important—as "reading freezes" was the acquired knowledge about thaws. If ice was newly frozen in a cold snap it was safer to venture near to shore—ice was more likely to "prove" there first (and if it gave way, better to be waist-deep with blades stuck in muck rather than be flailing away in deeper water in desperate straits). Of course, when first venturing on a river with unproven ice, whether initial freeze or refreeze-post-thaw, what was always most thrilling to see were fresh skate marks left by someone *else* who had already dared to venture, and had done a lot of the "proving" work already. (I could then just follow his trail!) However, given a good hard freeze and proven black ice, when a thaw would set in (depending of course on the type of thaw, but that's another story), shore ice would likely be the first to be compromised because of the conductivity of heat into the ice layer via shore growth, downed trees, bridge buttresses, and the like. Under such circumstances it was still possible to have excellent, safe skating over deeper water even while things were becoming dicey nearer in.

In addition to learning the nature of thaws, there was also the matter of learning about "refreezes." Subsequent skatable ice, after the initial experience of a hard freeze producing skatable black ice, always involved some combination of thaw and refreeze. Sometimes a "base" of black ice six inches or more thick would be compromised by a warm spell, or a snowfall — but *how* compromised? Did a workable base of hard ice further down survive a thaw? Not infrequently this combination was compounded, in addition to a thaw, by a snowfall that in and of itself could be sufficient to close-out skating. Even the pressure of a heavy, damp layer of snow could generate enough heat to begin to soften hard surface ice and turn it to custard. So learning to "read" ice extended naturally into the larger realms of learning to "read" conditions — the endless play of freeze, snowfall (or, if the Fates were with you, rain), and refreezes of some description. Learning how to calculate, in a manner that approached intuition, the interplay of these parameters — all a part of the macro — was the essence of "reading" conditions.

A good melt along with precipitation could raise the river level dramatically. Often a refreeze following such an interlude would "open" a marsh to really good ice, even while the preceding thaw left, as yet, unrefrozen bands of open water in the river channel itself. Where the initial thaw after a hard freeze would first compromise ice close along a shore, the sequence just outlined resulted in the opposite conditions: good shallow-water and marsh skating with treacherous conditions further out.

So why do I go to these possibly tedious lengths to give you a sampling of "ice knowledge?" Well, to some extent this knowledge — this strange kind of wisdom — that I acquired through my contacts with Wilbur, and my own experiences on the ice as informed by my encounters with him, really describe how my becoming acquainted with Wilbur very gradually, over many years, developed into a friendship with him. And my friendship with Wilbur really becomes the larger part of this story that I have set out to tell.

This friendship, in a way, developed as a gradual extension of the familiarity born of numerous encounters. It was not, initially, like a relationship based on "human interest" in which getting to know another leads to a deepening of what is revealed, either autobiographically, emotionally or both. For very many years there was none of this, really. The friendship that developed was a relationship of reliable sameness between two people, each of whom placed a high value on the experience of being out on a river on God's ice, exploring here and poking around there, accessing areas of river that could only be reached at this time of year and by this means—on ice, with blades. It was a relationship between two souls, each of whom valued such an experience, and knew that the other did, as well.

VI

For the first twenty years—twenty-one winters—this was how it was between Wilbur and me: Hail, fellow, well-met ⇒ exchange of reports on conditions on the river ⇒ further exploring the river together or separately ⇒ going our own ways with a hearty wave. Our relationship was calibrated by the elements. There was no other timekeeper.

Over that twenty-year span, we encountered each other—and skated together—many tens of times on the Sudbury. And what thrills that river would serve up! There were freezes (never many, but even fewer with the passage of years) in which the ice was so thick and solid that one could skate with impunity—almost—anywhere on the river—including under one of the bridges (very, very rare).

Far fewer than two handfuls of freezes over that twenty years offered this level of sublimity. But the ones that did were etched for Wilbur and me. Pure joy. We would start north of Fairhaven Bay and skate on down to the Route 117 bridge, portage around it, continue on through some tight bends further south, then skate under a smaller wooden span connecting Sudbury and Wayland and on out onto a broadening section of river traversing a broad marsh of conservation land for another several miles, either "hypotenusing" the river bends by cutting across flooded, frozen marsh, or following the meandering river course way on down (with one more bridge portage) to Route 20 in Wayland, and then return.[1]

There were quite a number of freezes not quite at this level, although still amazingly good, when bridges were not safe to

---

1) There was even one freeze so good that, in addition to almost limitless expanse on the Sudbury, the Charles River in metro-Boston also opened up—and it was even possible to skate the bridges downstream from Watertown Square. On one memorable afternoon, I set out just below Watertown Square and skated towards Boston, passing under all the bridges (North Beacon Street, Eliot, Larz Anderson, Weeks [foot bridge], Western Ave., River Street, Boston University [both railway and roadway], Mass. Ave. [the "smoot" bridge] and Longfellow [subway and roadway bridges]), in the process traversing the broad bay all the way to the wooden pylons to the right side of the channel near the Museum of Science leading to the canal locks—and back out again. (Regarding skating on the Charles, there is even a picture of my older brother Franklin and me on opposite ends of a line of five hand-holding skaters—we met the other three out on the ice—playing "crack-the-whip" by the Weeks Foot Bridge. This picture was run on the front page of the *Boston Evening Globe* on January 14th, 1971. I'm the guy anchoring down the line on the left side of the photograph.)

venture under. Passing drivers (if Wilbur and I had neglected to bring along our skate-guards to protect our skate blades while crossing pavement) would occasionally be treated to the spectacle of fleeting human forms on all fours semi-galloping across roadways—a weird sight, indeed! If we were prescient enough to bring skate guards, drivers would only glimpse two fully grown, allegedly adult males hightailing it across a roadway on ice skates (less strange, but still weird). These were our ways of portaging bridges and the open water often around them. Given this method of circumventing bridges, large expanses of skatable ice were still there to be had. Perhaps "the ice is always blacker on the other side of the bridge!"

More often, however, winter freezes of more modest scope would open sections of river, joys unto themselves, and Wilbur and I would check out the state of local muskrat and beaver lodges and dams. Somewhere along the line (was it after ten years? . . . or fifteen? I don't remember) we exchanged phone numbers. Wilbur even began, every once in a while, to call me (I lived in the city) to let me know that "the ice is in." My schedule of daily life was remade on the fly whenever I got *that* call!

VII

Up to this point (the fifteen-to-twenty year mark), there had been no calling—no need—to learn more about Wilbur in the sense of personal biography. I very briefly had met his wife Vivian on the ice a handful of times over these years, and had seen Wilbur with what looked like grown-up children. During the earlier years of my knowing Wilbur, I had had a career as a jazz musician and had made a few record albums (vinyl, in those days) that were finding their way out there in the world. Wilbur and Vivian learned about this through a neighbor's son (who just happened to have purchased one of my albums which he had found in a "cut-out" bin in a record store in Northern Maine). Wilbur and Vivian introduced me to him one day when he was out on the river with them, and he put my name together with the album he had bought.

As time went on, I started to become more comfortable on river ice—meaning I was developing some ability to read it. I had gained enough confidence to commence to take my wife out with me on river excursions. As children came along, I began to take them, though still young, out on the river when conditions were as safe as I thought they could possibly be (it's all relative on a river).

So there were these widely spaced (never arranged in advance) happenstances when various combinations of "me and mine" would, however briefly, encounter various combinations of "him and his." To call any of these chance encounters a social happening would really be pushing it, because they were merely what happens on an ice-bound river in winter: chance encounters between kindred spirits who hold in common a passion for the ineffable beauty and wildness of pristine winter-on-ice. The aesthetics of light-play—the play of pastels on ice—the winter skies portending further snow or freeze, the sunsets—my God, the sunsets!—the ice turning to gold or shades of pink as light from the lit-up bases of clouds, illuminated from beneath by an already set sun, would play upon the ice surface—an infinitude of segueing hues; the solitude of being so small in the presence of big sky and big expanse, the silvery half-light bliss of skating on moonlit ice in the thick of a most unyielding cold-snap—a full absorption into all of this left little need for socializing as most people understand the term. Ice is a great leveler; pretense need not apply.

So it was that in the winter of 1989, about twenty years into my acquaintanceship with Wilbur, there was a hard freeze in January that set up the river quite nicely, followed by a moderating (though still sub-melting) temperature that made it possible to get skates on and laced at river's edge without fingers going numb in a race against frost-bite. It was during interludes like this that I would pitch my family about having a "time on the ice." This always involved rapid rearrangements of plans, rarely more than twenty-four hours in advance. If ice was there, we had to catch it. Thaws and melting ice were no respecters of a slower response.

So on this day my wife and three children were with me, and my youngest, barely three years old (though she had little double-bladed skates of her own) was, for the most part, pulled along the ice on a sled. And this was the day when Wilbur happened to be out on the ice with Vivian and a few of their children and friends. And it was on this day that we, as families, kind of ambled and mingled a while, sashaying along bits and pieces of river. And it was on this day that in the middle of the afternoon it started to rain with some persistence, and everything started to soak through in a big hurry. And it was on this day that Vivian, impromptu, invited all of us back to her and Wilbur's house, about a ten-minute walk from the river, to "have some soup."

And it was in a conversation over soup that I happened to mention that many years before—August of 1972, to be exact—my wife and I had done some whirlwind, madcap driving through Nova Scotia, covering most of that immense peninsula in five days. On a Saturday afternoon, we had driven out to the beach and sampled the ocean waters off Inverness, Cape Breton Island, discovering, to our amazement and delight, that the ocean was, notwithstanding the northern latitude, *warm* at that place! I had said, that Saturday afternoon long ago, that I wanted, one day, to return to this region and explore it more fully. Now, sixteen years and change later, in Wilbur's and Vivian's living room in Concord, Massachusetts, Vivian, having listened attentively to my abbreviated account of that long-ago afternoon, said simply, "Oh, well, we have a place in Inverness."

Summer on Cape Breton—the sweetness of the season soothes this oft-inhospitable, but beautiful, coast. Photo taken along the MacKinnon's Brook Trail, Mabou Highlands, Cape Breton Island, Nova Scotia.

SUMMER

I

Sight Point Road was the road leading out of Inverness, Cape Breton Island, Nova Scotia, heading down the coast to the southwest, traversing the Mabou Highlands. The shoreline along the Mabou Highlands consisted alternately of a series of small ravines and headlands, and the "road"—an old carriage road from a bygone era—clawed its way along the slopes, etching out a fine filagree as it attempted to maintain a fairly level course while alternately cutting inland to loop along—to inscribe the inside bend of—a ravine, then swinging back out to traverse the next seaward headland—a back and forth dance of concave and convex curves. It snaked in and out and about those gullies, ravines and connecting headlands for a distance of eight miles or so. The road, on average, was perhaps 200 vertical feet above the Gulf of Saint Lawrence, a body of water large enough to be its own sea, fed by the Saint Lawrence River to the west, and opening to the North Atlantic between Cape Breton Island and Newfoundland to the east, and between the west coast of Newfoundland and the Labrador coast to the north. On the uphill side of the road were the Mabou Highlands, staunch, steep slopes of talus and scree, homesteaded by white spruce and occasional stands of hardwoods leading to tableland a thousand vertical feet above. Indeed, the slopes coming off the Mabou Highlands were very,

very pitched, forty-five degrees or more not being unusual. On the downhill side of the road, here and there dabs of pastureland and spruce forest sloped off and fell away to the sea below.

To the locals, Sight Point Road was known, and referred to, as the "Beverly Hills of Inverness." This was likely due to the fact that its occupants maintained homes and camps there that were obviously "second residences." It made no difference that these "homes" were often little more than glorified shacks. Given the harsh realities of an economy of coal-mines-gone-bust, *anyone* with enough money to maintain a "second" *anything* was considered well-to-do. The fact that many of the seasonal denizens along Sight Point Road came from the "lower forty-eight" probably accounted for the specific "Beverly Hills" moniker.

Along Sight Point Road, save for very occasional dwellings, now mostly seasonal—but, once, the year-around homesteads of little farms, dating from the late 1800s and early 1900s, that had been imposed, scatter-style, on those irregular, rough-strewn slopes—there was . . . nothing. Uphill the highlands stretched instantly into wilderness. Downhill, along with fields and forest, were stream-laced gullies and drop-offs to the ocean. At one time the carriage (as in "horse-drawn") road had actually been the connecting link between Inverness and Mabou, the next village of any size down the coast to the southwest, and the little settlements in between, long since abandoned and overgrown, of the stalwarts who had pioneered and homesteaded along this unyielding coast. The road had long since closed, at about the eight-mile point, to a dead-end due to recurrent rockslides along the steepest pitches of those rocky slopes. The rest was occasional hardwoods and ornery, wizened and ferociously tough white spruce. The road was, for most of its tortuous stretch, barely the width of one vehicle (to call it one-laned would give an altogether incorrect impression of its being paved). Its length and width were maintained by the passing through, at best once each summer, of a grader with blades tough enough to shatter ledge and to fill and restrew major upheavals and gullies that otherwise unceasingly attempted to reassert nature's own ideas about what constituted suitable landscaping and grading. This was the "Inverness" — the "Beverly Hills" — where Wilbur and Vivian took up residence in the summer months.

II

And so, seventeen years after happening upon it, my wife and I (now with children) returned to Inverness.

The Old Putney Camp was a fairly nicely constructed, if thoroughly abused and pilfered, little house at the very end of Sight Point Road. Once upon a time it had belonged to the Putney School in Vermont. Before that, it was a farmhouse. In its heyday the Putney School had used the house for summer-camp excursions by Putney students, alumni and faculty. Indeed, its heyday had likely included many "hay days," for as late as the early 1950s the surrounding slopes breaking way to the Gulf of Saint Lawrence were mostly fields — hard-won, hard-scrabble grazing lands seized from the stubborn spruce which, by the late 1980s, had retaken most of their lost ground.

The Putney Camp was actually the next-to-last dwelling on the road, and the last one directly reachable (if you were very careful) by car. It was the next house beyond Wilbur's place — the end of the line, meaning at the very end of that dead-end dirt and boulder-strewn road leading out of Inverness, bobbing and weaving its way on down the coast.

On the first visit to this untamed place the written directions simply said, "Keep going! If you feel like you should be there already, you aren't. You must continue until there is absolutely NO MORE ROAD. Keep going!!" On the walls and ceilings of the Putney Camp were messages blackened into plaster via butane lighters, appearing, strangely, not unlike a holding cell in a city jailhouse. "Peace, Love and diesel fuel" was one. Another read, "Are you waiting for the end? *This* is the *end!*" There were countless others of similar, cheerful reassurance.

The place was *wild*. On one of the maps the dead-end road was misrepresented as still connecting through to Mabou, the next major town down the coast. Indeed, as mentioned, once upon a time it had been the "through way." However, given the rockslides on those pitched slopes it had proven impossible and undesirable to maintain once the few settlements along it had dissipated. A connecting trail, where the former carriage road had narrowed to a body's width (very dangerous in spots) was all that remained. On one occasion during that first visit, a car drove all the way in, right up to the Putney Camp. The driver had been following one of those ridiculous maps, seduced by the unbroken line. He took the news of "eight miles in, eight miles out" reasonably well. Taking an additional moment to survey our site — our surroundings — the desolation, the view out over the Gulf of Saint Lawrence down through a narrowing old field closed in by ever encroaching white spruce, he just slowly shook his head. "I've got to hand it to you," he said. "I live in a rural area of New Brunswick, but I've never seen anything quite like *this*." Then he drove off.

I had some sense of foreboding about being so isolated. The local caretaker of the Putney Camp had a miscreant's reputation. (We'd been warned about him.) There was electricity (as conveyed along ancient, patina-coated copper wires supported by eroded, disfigured insulators along wizened, weathered wood poles), but no telephone. Once, many years before, while on a Boy Scout camping trip, I had been in a cabin that was attacked at 3 a.m. by a gang of rural town toughs—brick heaved through a window, shattered glass everywhere, and the scoutmaster using an ax to gash the wrist of one of the attackers who was trying to force entrance into the cabin—so I had decided, on this trip, to bring up my ham radio gear to see what links I could establish "just in case." I did make arrangements with a fellow ham in Charlottetown, Prince Edward Island (some 45 miles or so across the Northumberland Strait from where we were) to monitor a certain frequency that I would transmit on in the event that something untoward occurred. My ham radio acquaintance was glad to oblige. Had I needed him, he would have telephoned the Inverness Royal Canadian Mounted Police from Prince Edward Island (a very roundabout way to reach them!). As it happened, the "caretaker," who was *supposed* to know the place was rented, did show up late one night with some drinking buddies, already drunk, rowdy and ripe to continue a beer blast—and God only knows what else. I had, earlier, figured out a way to secure the entrances to the place reasonably well. Beyond that, with my wife and three small children to protect, I felt pretty defenseless. Fortunately, some terse words were all that transpired, and they left. But my ham radio, perhaps offering more an illusory sense of security than the real thing, stood at the ready. Thank God I didn't have to put it to the test.

III

There was a trail of perhaps one-quarter mile or so heading on past the outhouse, on through a little glen of Spruce, leading to Wilbur and Vivian's place. Their house was a more modest, less structurally sound dwelling, though much more lovingly nurtured and maintained and emended over three decades of collective ownership and seasonal occupancy.

Wilbur would come up to Cape Breton in early June, often accompanied by family friend Jean Rosner (who in years past had run a camp there, and still maintained a sizable spread along Sight Point Road). This early trip would be to get the gardens started, and to survey what vandalism had occurred over the winter. The road in was not winter-maintained beyond about the four-mile mark, so off-season, unofficial "residents" had places pretty much to themselves. Vagrancy was common, and there was always some vandalism connected with it. The Putney Camp's new copper plumbing, including the outdoor shower-head and small hot water heater, was lifted the winter after our first stay there. A friend of Wilbur's and Vivian's reportedly had both her stove and hearth stolen one winter. Wilbur's place usually had one or more shot-out windows and signs of forced entry and occupancy—notwithstanding a posted message welcoming off-season intruders and noting that the back door had been left unlocked for their convenience.

Having sown the garden and dealt with the consequences of seasonal vandalism in early June, Wilbur would come back down to Concord by around the middle of the month. The "season" up there really only got rolling around the second week of July.

Wilbur and Vivian would have vacated Concord by then, not to return from Cape Breton, in a typical summer, until shortly before Labor Day.

As we were settling in that first summer (1989) at the Putney Camp, Wilbur sensed that we felt we were in a bit over our heads. He and Vivian, however, were determined not to let us sink into any shock-induced lethargy as might arise from the primitiveness and remoteness of our surroundings, as unmitigated by high-tech distractions. The first full day we were there they showed up unannounced (the only way it could happen without a telephone) and announced that they were going on a hike up a trail to "MacKinnon's Brook." Would we like to go? The question carried, rather, the inflection of active encouragement rather than idle offer. So, still in a state of unacclimated stupor, we dropped our not doing anything, and went.

Wilbur was not one to gush emotionally about anything. He had a genuine warmth about him, but his style was not particularly demonstrative. He could be insistent, but his manner was easy-going and affable. So when he and Vivian stopped by to invite us on this hike, they in no way let on as to what we were about to see—what the experience would be like. Their abrupt descending on us was more in a spirit of nudging someone to "come in and get wet all over—Come on in, the water's fine!"—without specifying where the swimming hole was or what the water was really like. They wanted us to *participate*, and not by mild degrees. Our arrival at Putney Camp had already demonstrated that we had the wherewithal to *get* there. Now it was time to *be* there.

And so we followed these sturdy septuagenarian hikers along to MacKinnon's Brook. Without much by way of preview from

Wilbur and Vivian, we soon found ourselves hugging those 45-degree talus slopes, open to the elements and plunging precipitously to the sea, hundreds of feet below. The trail went through several stretches of "one-false-step-and-it's-'bye-bye'" terrain. And the beauty—my God!—such an unspoiled, untrammeled land/sea/skyscape! From the graphite filament of Prince Edward Island reinforcing the horizon to the Northwest some forty miles distant, to the rhythmic rising and falling of intersecting bands of ocean swell as viewed in patterns of infinite recurrence from our height upon the slopes, to the interplay of air, earth and water in some ceaseless, carefree dance—elemental wildness—to sights (and sightings), taken to be unexceptional in these parts, of eagles, harrier hawks, pilot whales, to sampling raspberry and blueberry delights along the trail. All this, plus warm-water ocean swimming where frigid MacKinnon's Brook meets the sea, greeted us, unhyped, as we followed Wilbur and Vivian that day. We had arrived; now we were truly "here."

With August visits to Cape Breton now a part of the mix, Wilbur and I, extending into the realm of "the Walworths and the Merrimans," gradually tapered on to a bi-seasonal relationship, and, in its own pace and rhythm, the summer one on Cape Breton was no less determined by the flow of Nature's offerings than was the winter one in Eastern Massachusetts.

IV

Wilbur's and Vivian's attitude about most things was "What is, is, and it doesn't serve to make much of a fuss about it." They had a near-perfect acceptance of the present moment—of whatever was going on or happening in their world—whatever that reality was. Wilbur would show up, chainsaw in hand, to make sure we had sufficient wood for our fireplace. (Knotty and stubborn, white spruce is famously difficult to saw or "work" in any way.) And they invited us for dinner—always a low-key invite—"Come as you are; anything you want to bring is just fine, but not necessary." Vivian created delicious dinners from their garden (which Wilbur had planted on that trip in early June). In addition to fresh vegetables, there would always be an array of spices and herbs, creatively blended, plus whatever fish or crab was locally available, followed by some form of pudding or dessert, usually featuring local berries. (Gooseberry pie was my favorite. Vivian had a certain fondness for gooseberries.) Inside, their house was more like a large shack, with weatherworn wood both inside and out, and floorboards that bowed easily under one's feet—sort of a springy, spongy feeling. The kitchen was built around a large, and I mean massive, wood stove.

Dinner always coincided with sunsets which, at that latitude, and with the sea's horizon to the northwest, still took place late in the evening (even though the summer solstice was pushing two months past). The extended twilight, migrating northerly along the horizon, would carry through most of the remaining evening.

How many dinners we had at that place over the ensuing years—how many get-togethers—I've long since lost count. Those gatherings always marked, for me, the height of our summer in Cape Breton. They would, on any given day, sometimes be preceded by a hike to MacKinnon's Brook, or expansive, leisurely times picnicking and skin-diving at "the cove," a local swimming spot at the base of a short, stout trail leading down to the mouth of a small ravine-lined brook.

V

An anecdote comes to mind that reveals much about Wilbur's temperament. Our second summer visit to Sight Point found us staying at a place called Port Ban, perhaps six miles up the twisty old road rather than eight. Wilbur was a good friend of the family that owned the place (the Hintons, Jean Rosner's brother's family) and would, of course, drop in to see how we were doing, and lend a hand as needed.

Wilbur could see the human dimension in any situation, both good and bad. He was not inclined to condemn, or otherwise take refuge in polemic or dogma (with one exception). He had few active dislikes, but the few he had were active, indeed. One of them was burdock, the plant that tends to, once established, take over an area via barbed, "hitch-hiker" seeds that latch on to fur or fabric with creative tenacity. It is said that the inventor of Velcro got his inspiration from studying burdock. Wilbur really had a distaste for it! Well, I spotted some growing around the house at Port Ban, and decided to take matters into my own hands. There was no cutting implement there that I could find, however there was a spade — a shovel — and I proceeded to wail on the burdock with the blade, turning it all into a pulpy mulch in about a half-hour's time. When Wilbur next happened by — it could have been later that day or sometime the next — he took a walk around, not nosily or anything, and when he came in, he asked matter-of-factly, "What happened to the rhubarb?" In a moment I was strickened to stunned silence. No one else knew, and I was too sheepish to say anything, and remained mute. "Oh, well," Wilbur said. It was all he said.

I put it together. On his spring trip up to Cape Breton with Jean Rosner, in addition to his own garden he had helped her plant the garden at Port Ban, as well as several others. And his efforts had come to this. I did get around to 'fessing up several days later, saying, "You remember, Wilbur, that rhubarb that got destroyed at Port Ban? Well, I mistook it for burdock, and had at it; I thought you'd be pleased about it. It never occurred to me that I was 'taking out' a rhubarb patch."

Wilbur just smiled slightly and said, "I figured it was something like that." There was no recoil or tension in his body, no emotional triggering or undercurrent of disappointment in his voice. He had put it together, and hadn't even developed sufficient resentment to have needed to corner the infidel, or to warrant forgiveness as an antidote. Knowing Wilbur, he had probably just wanted to spare me the embarrassment.

VI

The belching, gangling grader would work its way down the Sight Point Road, at most, once a year—often towards the end of the summer when its benefits would come too late in the season to do much good. But it was an exciting happening, nonetheless, taking several days to complete. Wilbur and his friend Jean would go out and "coach" the grader along, making sure that all the worst outcroppings of ledge and surface irregularities (it was all relative) would get their annual shearing. And no threading of the lurching grader along that road would be complete without the severing of various phone lines, water lines (gravity-fed from streams further up the slopes), and the gashing, squashing and crunching of collapsing corrugated culverts which had been placed at strategic points along the road to channel water under it (to reduce road flooding and washouts). Jean always appeared on horseback on those occasions, as if she might incite, via various war-whoop incantations, the waving of arms and feints of charge, the mechanized, snorting beast into doing her bidding. Various relatives spanning four generations would turn out to watch, and no other vehicular traffic could go end-to-end on Sight Point Road during those hours over the three days or so when the grader was at its work. The residents—year-round towards the Inverness end of the road, and summer denizens only along most of the rest beyond the sharp bend by Sherman's place—lovely little trout pool right by the roadside there—did not give the grader much more than a passing grade once the annual event was all over. The hangover of severed lines and gnashed culverts was not easily remedied. By the time these were tended to it was usually past time for the summer folks to head back to more southerly climes whence they had come.

Passing or failing grade notwithstanding—leaving the road, always, with sheared, yet still stout ridges of jagged stone stubble—there was yet a sense of awe that such a large, unwieldy belching beast of a machine could make its way on down that road to the very end, and back out again, *regardless* of whatever else it was supposed to have accomplished in the process.

Autumn—a red maple leaf, reposing on some weathered bark, makes, amidst it decline, a shameless display of its beautiful outline. Photo taken in Concord, Massachusetts.

FALL

I

There was often at least one presage of autumn that happened, by late August, along the northwest-facing coast of Cape Breton. A day or two would set in during which the wind would simply start to roar and howl, unimpeded, across the Gulf of Saint Lawrence, white-capping it up into a foaming fury. That northwest-facing shore would be its first obstruction after crossing a hundred and fifty miles of open water. The gale could be accompanied by horizontally driven rain, or, perversely, just drive onshore, pedal-to-the-metal-style, out of frigid, sun-drenched, cloudless cobalt-blue sky. (The sun held no warmth at such times.) Seas of twelve or more feet would surge ashore along Southwest Mabou beach, Inverness Beach, Belle Côté and Chéticamp, lapping right up to, and sometimes through the dune line, and "the cove" at Sight Point would have onshore surf break high over the jagged rock parapets, in the course of which surging streams of run-off would rearrange the whole contour of features that had seemed so solid, underfoot, and permanently established just a day before.

In Boston, had such weather paid a visit, it would have been front-page news. In Inverness, such a tempest was, matter-of-factly, referred to as "having a bit of a blow." The "bit of a blow" would pass, and the seductive lull of summer warmth would return, but notice had been served. By late September such "blows" would become more frequent, and soon thereafter come to own, and define, the place over the months to follow.

* * *

Back in Concord, in the relatively balmy climate of a Massachusetts September or October, Wilbur and Vivian and their children put on a party each fall for all their friends, and friends' friends. This was called the "Beast Feast." A yearling lamb, freshly slaughtered, was roasted over an open fire pit on a rotating spit that looked, to the untrained eye, as if it were cobbled together from old, random parts, including an electric motor, linked through a reduction gear via some bike chain to the turning rod, itself supported by makeshift brackets. Actually, appearance notwithstanding, the device had been thoroughly engineered, constructed and vetted by Wilbur's son Roger.

The Beast Feast was really an open house and potluck, happening equally within the abode and outside on the surrounding grounds beneath towering white pines and hemlock up against a steep slope to the rear of the house. People—very extended family and even more extended friends—would start to arrive the morning of the Beast Feast, and conviviality would extend into the wee small hours of the following day. There was an abundance of vegetarian offerings in addition to the heavy saddle fat of lamb, and a table full of creative, sweet confections of various sorts. An outdoor ball-and-claw-footed porcelain bathtub, half-filled with block ice, was otherwise laden with chilling beer and soft drinks. Tables were set up near the driveway with the sign "Not ready for prime time" placed upon them. People would bring serviceable items to give away, and would make their discoveries of abandoned treasures to take away from the discarded non-essentials of others.

Wilbur was always especially mellow at his big party. Completely mellow. He would be unshaven, dressed in a stained T-shirt, cradling a beer in his hand (Wilbur, the rest of the year, hardly ever drank), and would simply drink in whatever community of people were, on that given day, swarming over his digs. Any number of people who had met at past Beast Feasts and established cordial relations would re-encounter each other there (not having seen each other or otherwise been in touch in the interim) and resume acquaintance as if there had been no lapse. Connecting links for folks included Cape Breton Island, The Polaroid Corporation (where Vivian had worked as a research scientist with Dr. Edwin Land), a number of old M.I.T. and Raytheon folks (where Wilbur had worked as an electrical engineer), and the "Sub-Sig" community, a group of outdoor enthusiasts drawn from the ranks of Submarine Signal Company, where Wilbur had worked on the development of radar during World War II. (The company later merged with Raytheon.) Also present were mycology enthusiasts (Vivian and Wilbur were avid gatherers of mushrooms).

Wilbur and Vivian's children and grandchildren, along with multi-generational friends, would also reconvene in Concord for this event, a number of them trekking in from such far-flung places as Alaska, Arizona and California, the Pacific Northwest, Northern New England, and Cape Breton. The atmosphere of the Beast Feast was, overall, unhurried, low-key festive.

While it was technically a rite of fall, I always saw the Beast Feast as a note of forthcoming winter—and ice . . . river ice.

No Beast Feast for me was ever complete without my taking a stroll down to river's edge by following a narrow road between a couple of clay tennis courts (on the right) and a tangle of vines of Concord grapes (on the left) on through a small stand of woodlands punctuated by overturned, grounded canoes on through to water's edge. There was a narrow peninsula to the right of an inlet (which, itself, had been dredged), and, upon walking to the end of it, one could, looking south, survey a tidy swath of marshlands and follow the river as it gently arced towards Fairhaven Bay.

Taking in such a bucolic panorama, the question would always arise within me, "I wonder what kind of winter it will be?" At that time of year (from mid-September to mid-October, depending on the given year of a Beast Feast), it was always difficult to grasp, in an environment of leaves ablaze against deep-flowing water, that the conclusion of a transformation sufficient to render the current setting virtually unrecognizable was only a number of weeks away.

II

The fall of my life set in some years following our return to Inverness in 1989. We had made a pilgrimage each August to Cape Breton. The get-aways there were total and absolute. Having spent two seasonal visits at Sight Point, we found a place to rent in Mabou, the next village down the coast, and took up the comfortable pattern of returning to what we knew year after year. These times were special. We especially came to love the vitality of the indigenous Cape Breton music scene, with each town having "ceilidhs" that would feature the remarkably agile, creative playing of a gifted, multi-generation array of musicians, all devoted to an uncorrupted, culturally distinct music highlighting heart-bracing fiddle playing, amazing keyboard accompaniment, occasional bagpipes, and step dancing. We shared many memorable evenings with Wilbur and Vivian, over the years, taking in ceilidhs that were held every Thursday evening during the summer in the large hall adjacent to the fire station in Inverness.

I had no impending sense of how completely and irrevocably my life was about to change. But change it did. I found myself, in short order, feeling my way along treacherous legal shoals, with my career under assault, facing the loss of nearly 80 per cent of my income. About two years into this protracted nightmare, my first wife and I decided to separate, a prelude to eventual divorce after a quarter-century of marriage.

As I still loved my wife and wished to cause minimal disruption to her and my children, I decided to be the one to move out. This was not an easy time, and my future felt anything but assured. As I thought about where to go — where I could settle in to live out — weather — this accursed siege, Wilbur and Vivian came to mind. This was in late winter, early spring of 1996. I called Wilbur and, over the phone, briefly outlined everything that was going on. I asked him whether he and Vivian might have room for me to come *stay* with them "for a while." At that early time I thought — hoped — that there was some likelihood that my then-spouse and I could work through our difficulties and reconcile — something we had managed to do once about twenty years prior. So although I was open-ended in my request to Wilbur, I inwardly hoped I was looking at months, not years, of separation, let alone divorce.

It probably took less than two minutes for me to present the essentials to Wilbur. He was not hesitant in his response. "I think it would be fine," he said. I parried, "I know you have to discuss this with Vivian first, and please take whatever time you need for this." I was, in my own way, trying to let him off the hook (I don't know if *I* would have wanted to have *me* moving in with myself, given my circumstances!). "I'll talk with Vivian about it

Vivian & Wilbur: a picture is worth 10,000 words in conveying the beauty of the bond they had forged between them. They opened their home to me for four years while I was undergoing mid-life torments. Vivian, ever since, has referred to me as "family."

but I just don't see any problem," Wilbur said. The following day, he called me to say that Vivian and he would both be "delighted" if I would like to come to *live* with them.

III

My departure from my family's home occurred in early October, 1996. My little second floor room in Wilbur and Vivian's home looked out across a slope of woodlands. I slept on a small bed, alongside some built-in storage closets containing fossils that Wilbur and Vivian had gathered while pursuing earlier life passions. I was, I believe, sleeping next to "crinoids" gathered in Crawfordsville, Indiana. Crinoids are examples of ancient marine animals that are plant-like in appearance, and the current specimens were at least 340 million years old. Wilbur actually gave me a handful to give to my children.

Notwithstanding Wilbur's and Vivian's opening their home to me, the loss of the daily rhythms of family life was difficult, painful and extended. I would arise a little before six every weekday morning and drive in to the city to make breakfast for my youngest child (the only child still living at home during the school year), timing my arrival to be just after my former spouse was leaving for her job. I would see my youngest one off to school—a small fraction of the earlier daily rhythm, but one I was determined to maintain, as my youngest child benefited from whatever continuity could be provided.

I also still had a consulting office in my former home and worked there in the empty house for a while. This was a sad, sad time. To live through the progressive withdrawal of intimacy and affection, to sink into a climate of increasing alienation, hostility and marginalization, to clasp at echoes of something familiar while being intruded upon by a certain bleakness—all this was very soulful and painful.

Very gradually (for I am the world's slowest adapter to change) I became more acclimated to my new environment—my situation. Wilbur and Vivian were so accepting of my comings and goings without intruding upon me or cornering me in any way. They invited me to join in gatherings of their extended family and were never annoyed when this was more than I could do. This environment held and contained me whenever I was there, notwithstanding that it was usual for me to leave early in the morning, not to return until late in the evening. And very, very gradually I began to adjust to a new rhythm of family life in this "new" family I had, in some aspect, first become exposed to some twenty-seven years earlier.

For one thing, Wilbur and Vivian were night owls, on often separate trajectories; they had separate television rooms and liked different types of programs. The late-night environment, when I would drive back out to Concord from my goings on in metro-Boston, was one of cordiality and warmth. Vivian would often ask me if I had had dinner yet (there was usually some left on the stove). Wilbur and I would typically settle in at his TV-watching post and get involved in whatever the Discovery Channel was serving up. This kind of easeful entry, repeated hundreds of times over the four years I lived there, created an atmosphere of open conversation, many in the form of "chapters" that would knock off at bedtime (2–3 a.m. on some nights), only to be resumed the next evening at midnight.

There were those evenings when I would lie down on the comfortable sofa bed by Wilbur's video observation post—the sofa was aligned perpendicular to the TV so I could stretch out fully in the down comforter-covered cushions and settle in. On those evenings when I would be first to the room (by happenstance, not as a race) and Wilbur would subsequently appear there, I would start to get up off the couch so that he could have the use of it (I knew it was his favorite place to be in his "video hearth."). He would instantly start to wave his arms in the air, as if to *forbid* me from getting up and ceding the couch to him, exclaiming in a raised voice, "Don't get up! Don't get up!" He did not want me to be favoring him in this way, although I would often insist on relinquishing the couch, nonetheless. These exchanges of banter on such points led to a deepening of our "knowing" what we could expect of one another. My frequent refusals to give in to his attempts to forbid me — as interspersed by those times when I *would* let him have his own way in this respect — were a part of our getting to know each other better.

Now that I was living at "the Walworths," a lot of trust was placed in me. Wilbur and Vivian went on one or two major trips a year. One fall it was to Tonga and Samoa in Polynesia, as I recall. Another time it was Alaska. They were very interested in the natural world and ecology, and especially knowledgeable in the area of mycology. Spring would see many field trips to find and gather morels and other varied species. Wilbur also kept between forty to fifty plants indoors over the winter and they were "friends" to him. Near the head of Wilbur and Vivian's bed was a certain fern that had been with them through their fifty-plus years of marriage. There were plants from Southern Africa (where they had visited) as well. Wilbur lost track of how some of them had come to be in the house, but he was very clear with me that I was to take their "care and feeding" seriously when he and Vivian were away. I was nervous about this. After all, I knew (and I was sure about this) he hadn't forgotten that I had "taken out" the rhubarb. He "walked me through" every plant in the house—I think it was along the lines of making formal introductions. Notwithstanding his longstanding relationships with them and their importance to him (and my tawdry history with the rhubarb), he assured me, despite my jitters as a thoroughly non-proven green thumb, that I would do fine.

And I did! New sensory capacities started to come alive in me as I began to "read" a plant's condition by thrusting a finger into its soil. It just started to come to me that there was a correlation between the amount of soil, size of pot, amount of foliage happening, the climate in the room (depending on the season of the year) and the frequency with which moisture would need to be replenished. Some plants were always thirsty, while the peyote cactus would get a thorough soaking once in a blue moon. I had had earlier episodes in my adolescence of downright delinquency, and the specter of shame-laden revelations of unmet responsibility haunted me as I sought to caretake Wilbur's "friends." I can't really say that I was good at it, but at least I was not derelict, and my efforts seemed sufficient. I always breathed a sigh of relief upon Wilbur's return from far-flung destinations, in the absence of any obvious upset over the condition of his plants. After a few years, and with a few years of being in residence yet to go, I developed a reasonable confidence (a bit on the short side of "competence") and plant tending integrated into the flow of life there without undue anxiety.

IV

It was, I believe, in 1998 that Wilbur, while at Cape Breton, slipped and fell and suffered a puncture wound to his left eye. A sharp, jagged stick got him, and his eye was pushed back very noticeably into its eye socket. There was a hasty trip to New Glasgow, a sizable town on the mainland a little over four hours away, in search of immediate assistance, and then a follow-up trip to Halifax, some five hours or so by car, on the same mission. There clearly was considerable insult to the eye, and the only place that would be up to treating such a difficult injury (to the extent that such an injury was treatable by state-of-the-art measures) was in Boston. What I remember about Wilbur in those days prior to his return to Boston was his calmness. He wrote the whole thing off to his own clumsiness in having slipped and fallen. That was all. There was nothing much more to make of it, according to him. Never one to complain, his lack of complaining was not feigned. He just "didn't go there."

Surgery in Boston was somewhat helpful, though the injury was serious. The parallax was generally OK, but Wilbur could only see double in some positions, and the vision in his left eye was blurred. Wilbur adapted by disregarding the neurology of vision relating to the left eye. As time went on, his eye emerged, somewhat, from the deeper recesses of its eye socket cave. He regained most of his functioning and, indeed, that winter, we skated together and checked out the beaver lodges on the northeast corner of Fairhaven Bay. He was making do remarkably well, I thought. Vivian was a great comfort to him in rallying to obtain proper care for him, first via the more meager offerings in Nova Scotia, then subsequently back in Boston. Later I commented to him, in Vivian's presence, how devotedly she had sought to secure him aid during the most uncertain, unstable times immediately following his injury. He smiled, regarded her lovingly and, lapsing into the vernacular, simply said, "Yeh, Vivian done good."

V

Wilbur had few outright faults. There was the attitude towards burdock, to be sure (despite the fact that the cooked root of burdock can fare quite nicely in a salad). Wilbur just had no use for it. He was also very concerned about the consequences of overpopulation, and, more generally, the consequences of exceeding sustainable limits of any sort. However, his ruminations about this were always through the observant eye of a secular humanist as well as one who had received a thorough indoctrination in the scientific method. His views were rooted in ecological science and concerns over quality of life, rather than political commentary. He didn't see solutions to the problem of overpopulation or exceeding other sustainable limits, but he did, ruefully, see consequences.

Wilbur, as a man who was both very rational and very pragmatic, was also given to a quite definite atheism. Somewhat paradoxically, he and Vivian had met, over a half-century before, at a Presbyterian student-group meeting while attending the University of Michigan at Ann Arbor. Even secular agnostics have been known to pray "to whom it may concern," but Wilbur, as far as I knew, had no prayer life as organized in any form of ritual. He loved nature and, arguably, with the eye of a scientist, was quite a gifted naturalist. He "believed," if I can call it that, in the dignity and good will of all of humankind. To say he believed in this is not quite the way to put it, for Wilbur was not philosophical about it. He had no organized credo that I knew of. Rather, what we might call belief is simply an abstraction of how he actually *lived*. He was decent to everyone, without favor or neglect. He volunteered, one day a week for many years, to participate in an "inside-outside" discussion group at the local minimum-security prison facility in Concord, helping to publish a prison newspaper. He was a vocal advocate for reform of the penal system, especially the issue of giving prisoners a larger voice in decisions affecting the conditions in which they live.[2]

A non-exceptional example of his solidness in extending himself to others in this unheld-back way is revealed in the following anecdote. At the very end of 1998 I met Emily, and we began a courtship. I hadn't really expected to "meet" someone. For quite a while I had felt like the emotional equivalent of "road-kill," and therefore was not inclined to believe that I had a whole lot of wonderful things to offer to a prospective partner. I had pretty much made my peace with this reality.

However, one day at about the two-year point Vivian pronounced that I had "been alone long enough," and I took this as a sign that I had better be open to new possibilities. I met Emily in early December, 1998—a beautiful, intelligent, poised and very smart woman (and now my wife!), and much younger than I am. I had to go through quite a recalibration to believe that she

---

2) Besides the prison discussion group, Wilbur sponsored several pre-release prisoners and work-furlough inmates. The "Willie Horton" affair, used (successfully) to pillory Michael Dukakis in his Presidential bid in 1988, resulted in the termination of most such programs, and first-degree lifers were subsequently transferred to maximum-security prisons. Undaunted, Wilbur continued to serve as "family" for Julian, a first-degree lifer, and another prisoner (name unknown) in M.C.I. Gardner.

could actually be interested in me, or that I "should" be interested in her. Well, Emily's and my courtship started to deepen and grow. She actually dared (and, dare I say, enjoyed), within those first few exploratory months, taking a walk with me onto snow-covered ice on the Sudbury one frigid, full-moonlit night in January. A good sign. She had teaching jobs as adjunct faculty at a local college and regular faculty at a writing school, and I would, once or twice a week, pick her up late in the evening from wherever she was teaching, and drive her home to her apartment in Arlington.

When my life was falling apart in the mid-1990s, I had commenced a practice in psychological counseling (the field I had been involved with for many years) in Shelburne Falls, Massachusetts (about two and a half hours west of Boston). I needed a place to go to "lick my wounds," search my soul, and otherwise contemplate what was to be done with me. The routine developed in which I would travel out to Shelburne Falls for one or two days each week. A practice kind of fell into my lap almost from day one, so I had clients to see there. Some Wednesdays (my typical Shelburne Falls day), I would arise a little before 6 a.m. in Concord, get in to Newton by 7 to make my daughter's breakfast and see her off, put in some office time in Newton, then head west to Shelburne Falls to see afternoon and evening clients, and then head back East, getting back into the Concord area sometime between 10 p.m. and 1 a.m.

I was driving a very old Dodge Caravan that had become unreliable—"dodgy." On the evening in question, a "Shelburne Falls" Wednesday, I had offered to get back East in time to pick Emily up at at the Alewife subway station in Cambridge by 10:30. I was on schedule (always with fingers crossed, with that car—it had caught fire on me not long before) as I set out from

Shelburne Falls. A short ways east of Greenfield, I noticed that the red light had come on indicating that the battery was not charging. Even though I had replaced it recently, I just knew the alternator was gone.

To conserve whatever juice was still in the battery, I drove on parking lights most of the way back along Route 2. So far, so good. Approaching the West Concord rotary (where the prison is located), I knew a "statey" would likely be hiding out, and that I would have to make a show of having full illumination while going through that part of town, else I would be nabbed. I dared put on the headlights—with a glow of about ten-candle power at that point—and the engine nearly died. It was running, but just barely, and I could not accelerate. Fortunately I had enough coasting speed to make it by the danger zone.

With the battery so drained it hadn't the oomph to fire spark plugs with the lights on, and with a deadline to meet re: picking up Emily at Alewife, I shut off all the lights to save what energy I could to keep the engine running. The cylinders started firing in their regular cadence, and I was back in business! By God, even if I had to drive in the dark, I'd make it to Alewife on time to pick up my true love—lights or no lights! (Crazy thinking.) I was the phantom menace for the next two miles on Route 2 that night, until at last I came to my senses. I was approaching the intersection where I would normally take a right on Sudbury Road and proceed to Valley Road where Wilbur and Vivian lived. Snapping into awareness of how much of a menace I truly was out there on the highway, I elected to take the right turn. No sooner had I done so when the remaining juice in the battery was used up; the engine just upped and quit. I had enough momentum to roll to a stop on the shoulder of Sudbury road. I was a mile and a half from Wilbur and Vivian's, and seventeen miles from Alewife. It was 9:45 p.m.

I ran the rest of the way to Wilbur and Vivian's and outlined my situation to Wilbur. He, without hesitating, reached into his pocket for the keys to his Trooper and tossed them to me saying, "Bring it back to me some time tomorrow." He did not do this to ingratiate himself to me at all. This wasn't his nature. He did this because this is how he was. The situation required the use of a car; he had a car he wasn't using. That was all. The gesture was not "generous" in a self-conscious way. It was generous as a spontaneous outpouring of his availability to be of assistance. I picked Emily up at Alewife, on time, and returned the Trooper to Wilbur the next day. Yes, we were friends, but I never knew anyone who knew Wilbur who couldn't say the same thing regarding their experience of him, with equivalent "demonstrations" of Wilbur's unflinching assistance to draw on.

VI

Back to the burdock. In addition to this despised plant, there was one other area in which Wilbur exuded an inflexibility, the staunchness of which was noteworthy. I mentioned that Wilbur professed atheism. With the possible exception of the Unitarians (because of their climate of spirited, free-wheeling intellectual debate) and the Quakers (who he thought had "probably" managed to do some public good), he had no use for organized religion of any stripe. In his own way, Wilbur lived a version of the dignity of the common man: religion not necessary.

However, there was an inconsistency in Wilbur's scientific, rational, naturalistic, empirical approach to nearly everything. This was in the area of how he regarded anything related to "holism," "New Age-ism," or metaphysical philosophy, or any "claims" arising therefrom. For Wilbur, "New Age" was just a fumbled spelling of "sewage." Wilbur simply had no tolerance for anything having to do with this "pseudo-science."[3] He had long been a loyal subscriber to the periodical *Skeptical Enquirer*, which presents itself as a clearing house for allegedly rational (though often tendentious) gimlet-eyed skewering of all things loosey-goosey, holistic or "New Age." Wilbur and I ventured, now and then, into discussions about this. My temperament (based on certain phenomena I had witnessed, over the years, in my work as counselor and psychotherapist, along with a smattering of direct experience) was open to this area as a legitimate field of inquiry. However, Wilbur was adamant. Anything not lending itself to study via the scientific method was not worthy of study, period. I wouldn't concede this point to Wilbur, but I knew that any fruitful conversation in the wake of such a stern declaration was not possible.

I decided, however, to test Wilbur's attitude by presenting him a conundrum in which a certain "New Age" sensibility would combine with the possibility of replicable scientific observation, and see what he would choose to do with it.

---

3) The one exception to this rather monolithic bias was in the area of mind-body connection. In this area, Wilbur did recognize the validity of some research. He especially appreciated Herbert Benson, M.D.'s contribution, based on "good" (scientific) evidence. Vivian herself had participated in the hypertension program at Beth Israel Hospital and later at the Deaconess Hospital (both in Boston) where Dr. Benson worked. Providentially, I had also happened upon Dr. Benson's work in 1977 (see bibliography).

Many years earlier I had read a book called *Earth Energies*, by Hawaiian kahuna Serge Kahili King. (The book still occupies a respected slot in my library.) In one of the testable examples of a pervasive underlying energy postulated in the Huna tradition (roughly equivalent to the "orgone energy" of Wilhelm Reich), King set forth directions for making a "Manabox" for "collecting" this energy, by which its effects could be demonstrated. Borrowing loosely (and somewhat clumsily) on King's directions, I had constructed a little razor-sharpening Manabox using a plastic cassette tape box lined with a folded layer of copper flashing. Crude — *but*, my el cheapo disposable Schick double-edged razor got a new lease on life. Usually, I'd go through a razor in about a week and a half. With my little man-made Manabox I was getting (and continue to get), from each razor, clean, serviceable shaves for from six weeks to two months per disposable razor!

So . . . I made one for Wilbur, and presented it to him on his birthday (otherwise he might have refused it). Beyond the occasion of giving him a present (all wrapped and all) on his birthday, I presented my gift to him on purely empirical terms, saying that here was an apparent phenomenon in search of a theory (I told him about King's book.). He could, if he wanted, experiment with this "device" (no moving parts — copper slab within a plastic audio cassette case, no less!), perhaps making a chart and keeping track of how many shaves he was getting pre- and post-Manabox. I told him that as a disinterested party I would be curious to see what results he came up with, regardless of whether they confirmed or disconfirmed King's contention or my own findings. The worst outcome would be "no difference." The best: he'd save a few bucks on an ongoing basis due to not having to replace razor blades so frequently.

Wilbur looked at the little present with great suspicion and considerable unease. In that moment I saw that he genuinely (read: emotionally) did *not* welcome a chance to quantify something that was "New Age-y" — mysterious. In fact, he dreaded it. In this area his attitude was one of contempt prior to (and instead of) investigation. I believe I idly asked Wilbur on a couple of subsequent occasions — widely spaced — about whether he had "tried the razor sharpener." He hadn't. After his death, I found it, untouched, on the bottom shelf of the first-floor bathroom medicine cabinet, just above the sink.

Why hadn't Wilbur tried it? "Contempt prior to investigation" labels an attitude or predisposition, but in itself doesn't explain anything. Underlying such an attitude, I knew (from clinical experience), always lay fear. In Wilbur's case, I figured the common thread running through ideas embodied in such terms as "holistic," "New-Age," "ESP," "psycho-kinesis," was the possibility, no matter how unlikely, of encountering the occurrence of something sudden, unexpected, ungainly, upsetting, non-rational, unquantifiable — something unruly, perhaps untamable. What had happened to Wilbur to create and harden such an attitude? Here was a man I had followed across countless reaches of river ice, many of which I personally would *never* have ventured upon had I been out there on my own. Wilbur would just size up a sheet of ice beyond the point where I could trace the course of its "thinning," and move right onto and across it without any hesitancy. He "knew" (not quantifiable). More than once, trailing him on ice, I would simply stop short, my breath stacked in my throat, and watch him, following him only hesitantly even *after* I saw that he was safely across from one side of the river to the other. In all the years he had been out there on that river in all kinds of freezes, thaws and refreezes over countless winters, *he had never gotten wet.* (I would never be able to make that claim.) This was an environment where sudden, frightening, quirky, unquantifiable things could happen in any moment, yet *this* environment he had befriended. He had earnest respect for it, but it held no dominion over him.[4]

I formed a little theory of my own. It was simple. I figured that Wilbur had encountered a fright somewhere along the way, at an impressionable age when he didn't have the resources to digest it. I decided to try to find out. I don't remember exactly how I broached the topic, but I do recall my approach. I didn't link it to his attitude towards ESP or its derivatives, "pseudo-science" or the like. I came at it from an unrelated direction in casual conversation in which I mentioned some "frights" of my own. In fact, if memory serves, I didn't raise the topic with him by way of asking him outright. I "speculated," at first, about the effects that frightening experiences had had on me, and then kind of "wondered" out loud, "Hey Wilbur, I wonder if you've ever been freaked out, or encountered a fright at some point in your life?"

Bull's-eye. Wilbur went right to it. "I sure was once," he said, completely transparent, without a hint of restraint, nor note of suspicion as to just why I might be posing such a question to him. "I was walking down a sidewalk and a man jumped out of a bush behind me and just scared the living bejeezus out of me." Whether there was more to it than that, I did not inquire. He had volunteered this information freely and it was clear to me that this experience, as evidenced by the sudden force of his

---

4) Several years later, my wife Emily recalled Wilbur's actually having said to me on one occasion, "I know I took some chances on that river which, in hindsight, I never should have taken." What's interesting to me about this recollection (which I trust—Emily is an accurate reporter) is that, for whatever reason, I personally have no memory of it.

recollection, had had, one way or another, a pronounced effect on him. In a sense, he had "dealt with it" by erecting a barrier against the non-rational, however, he hadn't digested its emotional impact *as* emotion. I was reminded of an interview I heard with B. F. Skinner, the father of behavioral psychology. I had actually met him informally on a few occasions when I was in my late teens. His daughter and I were a part of the same social scene one summer (1965), and I had been at his house in Cambridge a few times — even played a few Bach fugues on the clavichord he had built and kept in the parlor. In the interview (I'm paraphrasing now) Skinner mentioned that he had no use for emotion. He had had a crush on a girl in his early teens, he said, and the experience had been so distressing and upheaving for him that he vowed never to feel that way again. *Never.* Emotion had to go.

I wondered, as I heard Wilbur share, in truncated style, his brush with fright, if an aftershock of this was for him to steel himself against having anything non-rational or emotionally "loaded" ever cross his path again.

VII

In October, 2000, I formally moved out of my room in the sanctuary that Wilbur and Vivian had provided me for four years. Emily and I commenced living together in Waltham. Actually, over the preceding year I had spent more and more time (and evenings) with Emily at her place by Spy Pond in Arlington. Our relationship had grown to the point where the next right step, in a sequence of right steps, was to make a home for ourselves.

However, I was still doing my one-day-a-week stint in Shelburne Falls, and Concord was en route for me. I would stop in to visit quite regularly, either in the morning heading west, or late in the evening when I would be coming back east. In other words, the continuity of my relationship with Wilbur and Vivian was maintained.

For two years following his injury Wilbur hung in there; however, the die was cast. I had noticed that his posture while walking was becoming more hunched over, and he was complaining more and more of losing muscle strength. Some sort of atrophying syndrome was setting in, and growing concern over the longer-term ramifications of a progressively degenerative disorder finally took the form of more formal inquiry.

Vivian took me aside one day while I was passing through Concord and told me that Wilbur had undergone tests for A.L.S.—Lou Gehrig's Disease—and that the test findings had been conclusive. "There is no cure," she said. "Wilbur's going to be in for a bit of a rough time." Wilbur would waste away unto death.

Wilbur and Vivian still kept at life at the pace to which they had long been accustomed. Vivian, in her "retirement," was the editor of the *Journal of Imaging Science and Technology*. In addition she was working as a consultant to a research and development group at the Rowland Institute for Science developing leading-edge stereoscopic imaging technology. Wilbur kept up on his reading, household projects and the prison group. They managed, as yet, a few more "big" trips—one was to Tonga and Samoa, and another was to Newfoundland to explore the Labrador strait. And, yes, they continued to go to their beloved Cape Breton.

That Beast Feast in September, 2000, found Wilbur his old, congenial self, hobnobbing (notwithstanding his hunched-up posture) at leisure, and with pleasure, with all his family and extended friends. That day Wilbur was as much himself as ever.

A month or so later Emily and I, newly moved in together, took Wilbur and Vivian out for dinner. This was a "thank you" dinner to them for having given me shelter and a loving sanctuary when most I needed it—a celebration, in a way, of a passage completed on my end. Although he was able to be out at the restaurant, both Emily and I noticed that Wilbur was barely eating—just poking at this and that, going through the motions. Nevertheless, this occasion was warm and wonderful. The stunning patterns of color on the turning leaves of the trees outside the restaurant seemed to capture the beauty of this gratitude meal on a warm autumn evening.

Yet Wilbur's decline was unmistakable. Within another month (November), mounting the steep stairway to the second floor hallway and bedroom had become very challenging. On a level space he was still getting around pretty well, and his temperament was buoyant as ever, but his physical-space—his physical world—was, by degrees, closing in on him.

VIII

As I would come through on my way to or from Shelburne Falls, I noticed that Wilbur was more and more often sleeping in the living room in a beloved (and ancient) black-upholstered reclining chair. Vivian subsequently bought him an even more comfortable blue recliner, and he gradually migrated over to it. The exertions of basic movement were becoming ever more taxing to him. He would be leaning back as far as the chair would recline, with his head extended even further back over the top of the chair, his face tilted straight upwards towards the ceiling. This was fast becoming Wilbur's "default setting" during the day.

However sometimes he was awake, still up and about, and quite conversational.

It was on one of those mornings, about mid-November, when I stopped en route to Shelburne Falls that Wilbur, alert in his chair, bid me sit down on the living room sofa adjacent to his recliner.

"Steve," he said, "I'm afraid I'm not going to be able to make it out on the ice with you this winter." I paused, nodding slowly, knowingly. "Wilbur, what can I say?" I responded. An instant gratitude attack came over me, and I found myself stammering, somewhat hurriedly to fill the empty space, "You've taught me everything I know about rivers and ice. I owe it all to you." Wilbur then paused, but he wasn't done. "I know that my condition is worsening more quickly than was forecast. I know I'm not going to be around much longer. I know I'm going to die soon, but I'm not afraid that I'm going to go to Hell or anything."

There, he had said it; he had broken the ice on death. The tone of his statements was serious and reflective. Following his lead, it was OK to talk about it. "Wilbur," I said, "I can't imagine anyone less likely to wind up in Hell than you." I smiled; he smiled. Not much more was said. We both knew that the topic of his dying had been broached, and that it was now on the table, and that we could, and would, revisit it.

How curious, I thought, that, as an atheist, he would venture into the territory of "not being afraid that I'm going to Hell." I guess, I mused, one can be atheistic — not hold truck with any god — yet still hold a notion of Hell in one's mind, even by way of dismissing it as an impossibility! Of course, it's possible that atheists, too, have their moments of wondering if there's "anything around the bend" (and even if there is, that does not necessarily entail a theistic conclusion). I've long figured that superstition is perhaps the most fundamental and primitive of unshaped religious impulses, and, god or no god, I'm reasonably sure that Wilbur still had the impulse. How curious, in a way, that of all the possible categories of concern that one might, as an atheist, have (and express) regarding one's own imminent death, Wilbur, whether dismissively or not, went straight away to a thought that contained the notion of a "hereafter."

IX

A few weeks later it was Thanksgiving. The Walworths had a gathering of family and friends. Wilbur, by this time, was spending most of his time in his living room chair, appearing comatose. If one observed the scene of Wilbur's semi-supine form arrayed across his reclined chair amidst a living room full of people, and took a mental snapshot, it would have appeared that he was dead asleep — not moving. Yet, this was not at all so. Stories were being recounted about Wilbur and Vivian's early courtship. There was one anecdote about how, while at Ann Arbor, Wilbur had gone over to Vivian's place to help her. She was, that day, intent on painting her bicycle and had called Wilbur for assistance because she couldn't get a stuck bolt to budge. He arrived on the scene and freed up the bolt, after which he suggested that she clean the bike frame with gasoline prior to painting it. He had given Vivian a ride on his bike (she sitting side-saddle on the crossbar) to the gas station to get the gasoline. Once the solvent had been procured, he had taken off, leaving her in the lurch to walk back home alone, carrying the gasoline in an open soup can. "I was pretty sore about that for a long time," Vivian said, "In fact, I *still* think he should have walked me home!"

Upon this recounting of an obvious miscue in courtship, Wilbur, a moment prior appearing comatose, suddenly opened his eyes, completely alert, smiled broadly, and, given that his voice was very weak and couldn't be heard in a room full of people, kind of superciliously shrugged his shoulders as if to say, "Hey, what can I say? What was I to do? She's probably right." He had been completely alert and relishing the story the whole time.

Everyone laughed. There were several rounds of this. One anecdote had to do with Vivian's father's advice to her regarding Wilbur. He did not favor the match. Regarding Wilbur, what it all boiled down to for his future father-in-law was: "Anybody who's that good-looking, you can't trust him!" Again Wilbur's eyes opened amidst what looked like a comatose state. There was the raised head, the grin, the hunching up of the shoulders as if to say, "Well, how could I do anything about that? He was probably right." The mirth which continued to abide with Wilbur through his illness, as evidenced by these examples (among many others), right up to the end, I shall never forget. That particular evening was, for me, a highpoint of the 2000 Thanksgiving-inaugurated holiday season.

X

In mid-December, 2000, Wilbur developed complications of pneumonia. His breathing was becoming labored, and the inability to clear his lungs was taking its toll. He was at first hospitalized on the critical care unit of Emerson Hospital in Concord, where he stayed for about six weeks. The plan was to stabilize him — or to experiment to discover what would, after which he would be transferred to the rehabilitation unit of MetroWest Hospital in Natick. I did not visit him while he was at Emerson. He was very uncomfortable and things were touch and go. He had a tracheotomy and the insertion of respiratory apparatus precluded speech.

When I heard he had been transferred to MetroWest, I decided to go see him there. I called Vivian to see if she was OK with this, and she was. As it turned out, our paths happened to cross in the hospital parking lot and she led me up to his room. He was looking very thin, hooked up to the usual array of beeping monitors, breathing (on oxygen) with difficulty, and his voice, though still audible, was slight. His speech was slurred — not from the effects of medication but as a consequence of the tracheotomy. He was, however, able to communicate verbally.

As I walked in I witnessed something I was to notice several times more before Wilbur died. I don't know if the experience was at all unique to me. When he saw me, he suddenly became almost radiant in an experience of pure delight. His eyes seemed to twinkle and a look of happiness and utter contentment came over him. This was an extended moment of pure glow. Any reservations I might have had about there being anything off-putting to Wilbur about my seeing him in what, medically, could only be described as a diminished state were completely obviated by this obvious overflow of his love and affection for me.

And it gave me license to touch him. I would gently caress his forehead and his hair, and kiss him on the cheek and then on the head in a flurry of small kisses.

What to talk about—given that he no longer had the where-withal to uphold his end of a back-and-forth exchange? It came to me. I decided to present to him, if he were willing, a little orientation about death. I decided that I would tell him something of how death is presented in dreams.

Any psychotherapist (and anyone else) who ventures into the realm of dreams is knocking on the door of a vast abode of psychical activity. Therapists may venture there for personal reasons, especially if one's own dream-life becomes unaccountably vivid or unruly, demanding personal acknowledgement, recognition, and "entering into conscious relation" with it. There are major schools of psychology that honor dreams—for instance, psycho-analysis (Freudian) and analytical psychology (Jungian)—and there are schools of psychology that don't attach a primacy to them (as in rational-emotive therapy, cognitive restructuring, and behavioral modification therapies of all stripes).

I was one of those who had, earlier in life, been forced to reconnoiter and deal with the dreaming me (or is it "us"?). And while not, in any way, demanding obeisance to the dream world on the part of my clients (I had been working as a practicing psy-chotherapist for twenty-plus years as of 2001), I would, nonethe-less, assist my clients in their dream-work in therapy whenever they would enter the consulting room with a need to talk about it. Over the course of my clinical work with upwards of fifteen hundred clients, it had been my privilege to witness something of how the unconscious deals with the question of personal, bodily death—the apparent extinction of the "person."

So I decided—in this instance of Wilbur's being awake and alert, but now with only a small voice with which to haltingly, raspingly respond—to tell him, if he were willing to hear, what I knew about death as revealed through dreams.

Having initially, himself, broached with me, some three months earlier, the topic of his own forthcoming death, we had established a comfort level about discussing this reality.

And so I ventured, simply and to the point.

"Wilbur," I said, "I'd like to say something to you about what psychology has to offer regarding an understanding about death, as revealed through our dreams—our dream-life. Are you open to hearing about it?"

Wilbur nodded his consent.

"Well," I went on—and this surprised me—"First, no one really knows what the fuck happens, if anything, after death."

As I said this, my spontaneous gesture reached to underscore the apparent offhandedness of my remark. My shoulders kind of hunched up, and my lower arms extended out from my torso and jerked up slightly in synch with the expletive, with hands open and palms facing upwards.

What surprised me was my use of profanity. Wilbur was *not* one to use profanity. In fact, I don't recall ever having heard him swear. My own lapse into profanity, startling to me, was on some level calculated to keep the topic from getting too high-falutin' or heavy. In the glibness of this expletive, there was notice served that I was not going to attempt to corner him into having to believe, or concede, anything. Upon reflection about this conversation (and I have thought about it a great deal) I believe that I was, unconsciously, trying hard to keep the topic as safe as possible for him, given his strong, emotionally laden prejudices against "pseudo-science." My way of doing this was that I was just going to be reporting. That's all.

Again, surprisingly (and putting *me* at ease), Wilbur, leaning upright in his hospital bed, spontaneously gestured in a manner that mimicked my own. A quizzical smile appeared, his shoulders hunched, the lower arms went out and were raised, palms up. Wilbur's gesture was, loud and clear, "Yeah, who the fuck really knows?!" Wilbur was ready to venture further; he was ready to hear more. His mind was open; he had nothing to lose now.

And so I continued. "Well, here it is," I said, plunging in. "All I can really tell you is that at the level of dreams—in our dream-life—death is recognized as an event, but it is not recognized as the end of consciousness. I don't know, and can't really offer, a fuller explanation of why this is so, but the observations are there, both in the psych literature and as borne out by what it has been my privilege to observe in the dreams of many, many clients, some of whom have since died. So, even though no one really knows what the _____![5] is going on, that may not be the end of the story."

Wilbur took all of this in; he was attentive and interested. It was then that, again surprising myself, and without prior conscious intention, planning or anticipation, I logically extended my presentation to Wilbur in the only way I could.

---

5) The aforementioned gesture took the place of the utterance, the word's purpose via previous utterance having been fully realized.

"Wilbur," I said, "I have a favor to ask you."

"Yes, go ahead," Wilbur replied in a husky whisper.

"Well," I continued, "we both know that nobody really knows what happens after death, or at least after bodily death. Maybe there's something, maybe not. However . . . ," I paused, suddenly *fully* aware of where I was going with this, ". . . *if* it turns out, despite what may now seem the extreme unlikeliness of this, you discover that you are conscious — have awareness — after you're 'dead,' and *if,* within this consciousness, you should somehow ever get wind of the fact that I'm out there skating on the river and in danger — heading for a patch of thin ice or otherwise skating where I shouldn't be — and *if* you are in a position to be able to communicate with me by whatever means is available to you to warn me of this, would you be willing to make the effort to do it — to get through to me?"

There. It had all just tumbled out in this ramshackle manner, and there my question was, out in the open with nowhere to hide. On some level I guess I calculated, notwithstanding Wilbur's historical aversion to anything "holistic," "New Age" or loosie-goosie, that placing my request in the context of one dear friend coming to the aid of another would hook the side of Wilbur that was so spontaneously and reflexively helpful. I figured that framing my request in this way would likely meet with his consent. Still, it felt daring to ask.

Wilbur, however, did not hesitate. "Alright," he said, his voice a firm whisper, "I promise that if I'm able to do it, I'll do it."

"Thank you, Wilbur," I said, feeling both grateful and exhilarated. I gave him a kiss on the forehead and stroked his hair a bit. He was relaxed and seemed pleased and at ease with himself. I was very happy and exceedingly pleased with him.

XI

Wilbur was scheduled to return home from MetroWest in early March. All in all, between the Emerson hospitalization and the MetroWest one, he had been hospitalized for nearly three months. The home he returned to had been re-arranged. Climbing stairs was no longer possible, hence it was farewell to the upstairs bedroom. His video-hearth room on the first floor was remade into his bedroom. The room had been repainted and an adjustable hospital bed had been moved in. Also installed in the room was a full complement of respiratory equipment.

Vivian had been unsuccessful in lining up visiting nurse coverage to help her out at home. The liability issues were too daunting for any professional home-care organization to overlook, given Wilbur's progressed A.L.S. and his need to be constantly maintained and monitored on very imposing respiratory equipment.

But Vivian was determined to have him home, which is where he wanted to be. So, during his hospitalization, in anticipation of his return, Vivian and daughter Irene took a crash course in nursing care, including the operation of the respiration equipment. (There's a lot to it.)

And home he came. It was clear, home in his first floor room, that the former video-hearth abode would be Wilbur's last stop, or, perhaps, his jumping-off point. He could no longer speak and could barely gesture. His bodily appearance was extremely frail and quite emaciated. He was at Death's door. The one apparent contradiction to this that I witnessed the small handful of times I saw him in the several weeks prior to his death was identical to what I had seen in that hospital room two months prior. Whenever I would enter the room and he saw me, his face would suddenly grow animated and so expressive. His eyes would open seemingly to saucer-size, his mouth would assume a grin, his cheek muscles — what was left of them — would tighten, and his whole expression would lift into a glow of wide-open love and joy. He was just thrilled to see me, and he conveyed this to me with a fullness and immediacy that would have done justice to anyone with full physical faculties at their disposal. Once or twice I questioned whether my love for Wilbur may have distorted the pronounced effect I thought I was seeing — the "glow" — the ebullient radiance emanating from him when he would first lay eyes on me. Fortunately, however, on one of those final occasions Emily was with me and witnessed the effect herself, so I am reasonably sure that I was not deluded or otherwise hyperbolic in my assessment of what I was experiencing with him.

Following this remarkable display of love and greeting, I would just kiss him on the forehead and stroke his hair a bit, with an occasional gentle tousling of his white hair. In clock time — consensus-reality time — these visits were quite brief now. Encapsulated within the time-bracketed envelope of each visit, however, were moments of timelessness and tenderness. There was really nothing that needed to be said, or pass between us, that hadn't already been expressed. Our relationship, in thoroughly worldly terms, was complete. Nothing remained between us as unfinished. Wilbur would not be alive much longer.

With the final curtain about to fall on Wilbur's life, family gathered around. He and his family had been most generous to me in so many ways. They had treated me "as family" for a very long time. However, as I was no longer living at the Concord home (having taken up residence with Emily in Waltham), I faded, in those final few weeks, more into the background. It just seemed right. I knew that a call would come my way soon enough announcing Wilbur's death.

And so it did. Vivian called me. Never one to entrust a machine to faithfully convey a message of such weight, the message she did leave, on April 22, 2001, was simply "Hi Steve. It's Vivian. Would you call me please?" That was it. On returning Vivian's call, she reported that Wilbur had died a few days earlier, on April 20th. She said that he had indicated, a few days prior to his death, that going on was simply too much to bear, and that he was ready to let go. He wanted to leave.

Two months later, in late June, a memorial service was held for Wilbur at the Unitarian church in Concord. Vivian had already, in early June, made her first trek to Cape Breton without him, to get the garden started. She would return again in early July for the duration of the short summer there. Emily and I attended the memorial service, and it was packed—200 to 250 people perhaps. Moving eulogies were offered by his children. There was even an open invitation for anyone to take the podium and share something about Wilbur, ex tempore. I had a brief impulse to relate the story of my "taking out the rhubarb" and Wilbur's gracious display of forbearance about it, but I chickened out, and the moment passed.

Vivian and family had assembled many photos and artifacts from Wilbur's life, and these were on display in the reception room downstairs following the service. The event could not have been more full—a loving, overflowing tribute to this wonderful man.

Spring—a cluster of lily-of-the-valley lends an air of delicate fragility and gentleness to a peaceful, wooded hillside. Photo taken at Lake Waban, Wellesley, Massachusetts.

Spring

I

In mid-August, 2001, Emily and I headed to Cape Breton. Many years earlier, in December, 1991 I had purchased a Panasonic VHS camcorder to assist me with my work. Six weeks or so following this purchase, the Sudbury River, amidst a mid-winter freeze, had done its thing: a magnificent layer of ice was upon it. Vivian had called to let me know how good the ice was, and we had made plans to go skating the following day, a Saturday. I decided to take the camcorder out to the river to see what it would do.

That next morning the temperature had moderated and the sun was out—a perfect day to be out there on the river. My family had all come with me, and Wilbur and Vivian and long-time friend (from both Concord and Cape Breton) Jean Rosner, also had come out to play on the river as well. I made, really, quite a lovely video of all of us (including my two older children Hannah and Hardy, fast becoming seasoned skaters, and my youngest, Joely, who had her first pair of single-blade skates and alternated between shuffling around on them and being pulled on a sled). There was wonderful video footage of Wilbur on this tape.

Prior to driving up to Cape Breton I had reminded Vivian of the existence of this video with an eye, should she want me to, to bringing it to Cape Breton, along with a VCR and a monitor, so that she could see it. She was enthused at the idea, and so it traveled the 800 miles up from Boston with Emily and me.

On another of those amazing evenings when a spell-binding sunset was in the offing off Sight Point, and a delicious dinner had been crafted out of the local catch combined with fresh veggies from the garden, followed by the de rigueur gooseberry pie, Vivian, Jean Rosner (who had come over especially for the occasion), Emily and I sat down to watch it. And there Wilbur was, as vivid, animated and true-to-life as ever! As the video revealed, we all skated down through Fairhaven Bay and around the bend almost to the Route 117 Bridge. Damned if Wilbur didn't notice one dodgy patch of ice that could have meant an untimely swim if not seen in time. The risk was only subtly noticeable; he picked it right off. I never would have seen it. But his tone was not alarmist—no "Watch out!!!" It was more like "You probably don't want to go -----," or "You probably need to keep clear of -----." So typically Wilbur, the tone of assurance was part of the warning.

Near the conclusion of this time on the ice, with camcorder running, I dared to skate fast, non-stop, all the way from Route 117 on across Fairhaven Bay to the point of egress we used on the river—a distance of about two miles. I wanted, that day, to capture the sweep—the scope—of ice on that river, and I did so, without falling and smashing my new toy. All of this was there to be seen on this video.

Jean and Vivian thoroughly enjoyed this blast from a wintry past as it was shown in the sublime summer twilight in the Mabou Highlands of Cape Breton Island. That evening was full of fun and good cheer. I guess, in some sense, we had brought the spirit of Wilbur's video-hearth, along with those priceless images of freeze-framed vibrancy, to the Cape Breton he loved so much. In similar manner he had been able to be present at Cape Breton after all.

II

In September there was yet another Beast Feast in Concord — the first, of course, without Wilbur. Yet the laid-back ambience of multi-generational friends, family and colleagues was surprisingly similar. No break in this tradition at all.

Vivian was doing well. In some ways, Wilbur's passing was a relief — to her, to be sure, and to his family who had seen him suffer so with the debilitating effects of A.L.S. I was surprised to realize how seldom I thought of Wilbur. Strange that my thoughts about him, when they occurred, revolved around how I *wasn't* thinking about him! (Slightly perverse, this.) He was gone, and there had been nothing left unsaid between us prior to his death. It was a fulfilled relationship to which nothing more need ever be added, nor from which could anything be subtracted. It was complete. There was no space taken up with how things might have been different "if only" such and such had happened, and so on. No guilt; no remorse; no second-guessing.

Fall deepened into winter, once again (as it always does). I was stopping by the Concord home every two to three weeks or so while (as usual) en route to, or returning from, Shelburne Falls. Vivian seemed well occupied and accepting — no glumness. Perhaps she even felt liberated, after a fashion.

In January my phone rang, and it was Vivian. "Stephen," she said, "the ice is in, and I've been thinking about going skating and wondering whom to call to go skating with, and I'm calling you. Would you take me skating?" When I got out to the house later that day, she explained, "I always used to skate with Wilbur, and I never had to worry about whether it was safe or not. Now that he's gone, I figured you'd be the person to call."

I felt very honored. Here she was, asking me to fill Wilbur's skates—to take her skating in a manner that would guarantee her safety the way Wilbur did—without her having to worry about it. I was kind of nervous assuming *that* level of responsibility but, as I have said, honored that she would ask. I figured Wilbur would approve.

So we went out!—Vivian, pushing into her eighties, and me in my mid-fifties. We made our way very carefully upriver to Fairhaven Bay, and then over to the far shore on the northeast side, and then into an inlet, crossing the low, wide beaver dam to scope out the beaver lodges. Looking back, I realize that Vivian and I retraced the course that Wilbur and I had taken the last time we ever skated together. Vivian was wonderful on the ice—still sturdy and strong. The whole time I was with her that day I felt, as I read the ice and kept us moving yet safe, the priceless inheritance I had received from Wilbur—how to read a river, how to read ice, how to share in, and partake of, nature's bliss in the presence of people whom you love and who love you—how to hold as a sacred trust the experience of a timeless friendship—a friendship that exists outside time—sourced in mystery and fulfilled in so many ways, great and small, including accompanying and providing safe passage for his beloved spouse and soul-mate.

Like so many experiences involving Wilbur, this one was complete. It would be presumptuous of me to proclaim that Wilbur's role as "river wizard" had been passed to me, but on that day at least, I acted *in loco Wilbur* in a manner that I think would have met with his liking. And Vivian really enjoyed herself.

III

At this point in my narrative I must digress, considerably, in order to provide a context for faithfully reporting what was to transpire over the following few months. But I promise I shall return to it.

I have made earlier mention of the respect I have for dreams—and our dream-life while sleeping. My own dreams strike me as unexceptional. My dream-life is fairly sporadic, and I am often too lazy to record it or attend to it properly. Yet there have been times—even quite extended periods—when I have been faithfully attentive. These more extended times have sometimes occurred in concert with psychotherapy which I have sought out for myself, and at other times when I have been on my own, sans therapy, and something has shaken loose in my psyche that demands attention, but can only gain it by giving me a "gut-shot" while dreaming—something specific and acute enough to jar me into conscious recognition. To say that I do not regard my dream-life as "exceptional" is not to downplay the importance in which I hold it. My dream-life is unexceptional only because, from what I've seen, *everyone's* dream life has it within it to be, if attended to, equally "exceptional."

So what I must first report along these lines goes back to about 1980 or so. Over a period of several months I had a series of "dreams," the likes of which I had not, to the best of my knowledge, previously encountered.

In the initial dream in this series I was trying to fly, involving quite vigorous effort, and was managing to lift, very arduously, a short way off the ground. At some point something happened within the dream that was unprecedented for me. I became aware that I was dreaming—which is to say that I became fully conscious with my everyday, wakeful consciousness at the point of "lift-off."

As this happened, rather than realizing, as "awake," that I was lying in bed, a panorama in full, three-dimensional living color suddenly unfurled, almost like looking through the widening aperture of a motion picture camera lens. I was hurtling through space—down a boulevard—at about telephone pole height (I know the height because I was "flying" right past them!). The colors were completely vivid and I could feel the wind in my face. It was a total immersion—with my being in possession of my everyday, wakeful consciousness—in some remarkable, almost kaleidoscopic reality.

What shook me out of it was the lag-time reaction of shock, as it dawned on me, awake in my dream, that this experience was actually happening. It was the "startle" of this recognition—the adrenal "fight, flight or freeze" reaction of my own endocrine system and its attendant neurology, that closed down this brief, fully conscious encounter with whatever that reality was. It was only then, with the memory vivid and my train of consciousness still unbroken, that I "referenced" myself as being in bed, with my wife sleeping soundly to my right.

The exhilaration of this vivid experience was tempered, over the following day, by my ruminations about whether such a happening could be presaging the onset of some form of mental disorder—possibly even a psychosis. I shared this concern with my then-spouse. I was also in psychotherapy at the time, and managed to tell my therapist about the experience, along with my attendant concerns. Over the following several months one handful's worth of additional experiences occurred. The trigger in all but one of them was the act of arduously, with bare, yet definite, initial success, trying to fly, and then something in the "lift-off" stage would make me "awake" in my own dream and it would all just kind of unfurl and roll on out; my tethers were momentarily unshackled. Then would come the slightly delayed awareness that "Whoa, this is happening again!"—the reaction-to-the-reaction, so to speak—and this reaction-to-the-reaction (involving a shot of adrenalin, I figure) would jolt my neurology in a different direction, and the "dream" experience would close down—*but consciousness would not be broken.*

In the one other dream in this small series, the vivid aspect was non-visual. In this dream, as I became aware (wakeful consciousness) I felt, as a complete kinesthetic experience, that I was rolled up tight as a ball, at which point I experienced the most colossal acceleration my body-bound consciousness has ever knowingly registered. I was hurtling through an undefined volume of space at unknowable, yet colossal, velocity, the acceleration of which continued for what seemed a surreally long time.

So there was my unheralded series of vivid dreams, and the experience—as I was later to hear it described—of becoming "lucid" in my dreams.

With each recurrence of this type of dream in this brief series, I continued to worry. It would be several years before I happened across Stephen LaBerge's book *Lucid Dreaming*, in which he set forth some of this territory more formally. I had already read Robert Munroe's *Journeys Out of the Body*, so I knew that out-of-body experiences had been reported and that there was a literature about them. So, by way of having a minimal concept through which to consider these experiences that were, unbidden, arising in me, I was not quite completely in the dark. Still, I was worried for my sanity.

And then, as quickly as this series of lucid dreams had arisen, they, by and large, ceased recurring. I would have them only very sporadically thereafter—and very infrequently. This was how it was for the following twenty years or so. To the extent that I could attach "meaning" to them, all I could really surmise is that they—the original cluster—served to awaken in me an awareness of one of consciousness's capabilities. I knew at least that one could have convincing, utterly subjective (and unprovable) experiences of apparent alternate realities as perused, and participated in, by everyday wakeful consciousness. Yet with this kind of experience becoming so much less frequent after the first few months of this epiphany, I really could see no sense to them, and their occasional recurrence remained a mystery. Eventually I came to regard them as a benign enigma.

I should also mention, at this point, that although I had been a heavy drinker of alcoholic beverages (and otherwise light substance user) in my early twenties, I had not, as of the time of this startling dream series, consumed any alcohol or used any psychotropic substances (with the exception of caffeine in tea or coffee) for more than nine years.

IV

It is time to return to my narrative.

On the evening of March 24, 2002, I had another of those very infrequent, lucid dreams. It had been at least several years since I had experienced one of them. In many ways this dream/lucid experience was the strangest I had encountered up to that time. I include the dream here because it may or may not have a bearing on what was to follow. Here is a transcription of the dream, taken verbatim from my dream journal:

> I am by a village square—train tracks and grade crossing to my right. There is this band of energy—electrical—that is approaching—that radiates perpendicular to the tracks (in the horizontal plane)—and across them. The waves/bands of energy look very powerful. It may or may not be like the radius of a center—sort of spoke-like, or it may just be a plane moving forward uniformly like a wave front. I wonder what effect the wave—traveling broadside about 18 inches off the ground—will have on the crossing-gate housing in its path. As I continue to watch, it just passes through it as if it weren't there—no discernible effect on it. As it approaches me, I figure I can jump up and over it, even as I see yet another one traveling behind it, in its path.
>
> My attention is drawn to the visual field on my left in which a multi-colored bundle of energy is moving around in free space. As I watch it, it draws nearer to me, then suddenly penetrates my head and is inside my brain, or so I perceive it. This startling occurrence is followed immediately by a series of high-pitched sounds, of various frequencies, tonalities, and "bursts"—non-recurring rhythmic sequences—in which I experience my brain as being rewired, reprogrammed, or

subject to a remarkable array of precisely calibrated neuro-logical adjustments, tweaks and fine-tunings. As this is happening, the dream is vivid, and I'm totally 'tuned in' to my head, brain, astounded at the precise, unhesitant nature of the tunings. It's as if whatever has entered my head/brain/ neurology knows exactly what to do/go for, and is amazingly efficient in carrying out these operations. (What a blueprint of my brain/mind this energy must have!)

I awaken feeling some excitement to have been so visited, with recollection so intact and sense so vivid.

Although it is not my purpose, at this point in the book, to comment specifically on this lucid dream, I have wondered whether it was seminal in what was to follow. While, to this day, I can't be sure, its occurrence nevertheless seems salient enough to warrant inclusion in this narrative. Do note, however, that in the recording of this dream there is no mention of Wilbur, nor any apparent or intrinsic connection to him, either within the dream itself, or in my wakeful reflections about it immediately following.

So here is what happened. On the morning of April 15, 2002, at 4:15 a.m., Wilbur paid me a visit. I had gone to bed at my usual hour—typically around midnight or so. Emily, my partner (and wife-to-be), was sleeping to my right. I had had no particular thoughts of Wilbur for quite a while—at least weeks, possibly months. Since his death almost a year earlier, I had, if memory serves me at all well, not ruminated on the deal we had made with each other when he was in that hospital room some fourteen months earlier. To the extent I had reflected on Wilbur's death it was in a spirit of loving reminiscence, untinged by feelings of regret, remorse or there being anything "unfinished" between us. Or, as I have mentioned, occasionally he would pop to mind and I would, paradoxically, note how seldom I was thinking about him. I don't recall, since his death, ever wondering whether he would pay me a visit, or otherwise "get through" to me. But he did.

Here are the verbatim transcriptions from my journal:

4-15-2002 4:15/20 a.m.

Wilbur came to see me this a.m.

(This entry was intended to log the event, establishing that the occurrence had happened. I would have written a fuller account of it at the moment; however, the experience of the visitation was so full and rich that it left a remarkable afterglow, which I wanted to savor fully. I was afraid that writing it out in the requisite detail would prematurely truncate the experience before it had subsided on its own. I didn't want to intrude upon the experience's natural rhythm by making it bend to my need to record it.)

The experience was so powerful and far-reaching that it seemed etched in my neurology with a vividness that did not lessen over the passage of several weeks. I was constantly engaged with it. By the end of May, 2002, I had reconnoitered the experience sufficiently to attempt the unavoidably awkward translation of it, a living reality, into the straightjacket of linguistic expression.

What follows is the verbatim transcription from my dream journal:

Transcribed on 5-29-2002

Recount of Wilbur visitation on 4-15-2002

There was this gathering at a house that is, loosely, Wilbur and Vivian's. It is in Concord.

The gathering—a commemoration of Wilbur—is to feature a reading, in which a number of us are to take part, of a 'manuscript' in the form of an assemblage of Wilbur's writings. A man whom I don't recognize—dark, short hair with a manicured beard—has done the cutting and pasting to create the manuscript/script. I know that a lot of work has gone into this, and feel impressed at the man's effort.

I am entering a hallway—have to step over someone who is stooped down at the threshold and (perhaps Vivian) calls me to assist in replacing a light bulb—a small lamp fixture protruding from the upper portion of the hallway wall. Having step (sic) (sort of) over the person/figure who is stooped (at a task) at the side entrance to the hallway (one step up 2 or 3 steps to this entrance) I climb the 2/3rd size stepladder in the hallway to reach the light bulb in the fixture.

It is then that my eyes are drawn to the ceiling (as if the hallway has expanded to become a sizable room), and there (upon) I see three oblong glowing, luminous, incandescent oval 'forms' along the ceiling—three in a row , the nearest of which has within it the unmistakable features of Wilbur's face. (!)

I am startled to see 'Wilbur' 'here'—I realize instantly that it is he—that he is actually coming in—present at this gathering. I realize that others don't know it.

It seems that simultaneous to my 'seeing' Wilbur, my situation changes from being up on the ladder to assist in changing a lightbulb, to having my part of the manuscript (Wilbur's) to read at a lectern—although now that I realize that 'Wilbur' is here I realize—faster than thought—that this is no commemoration to a deceased person—for he is with us!

At exactly this moment his energy—the luminous forms—come off the ceiling and enter me through the head region and surge through my entire body. The dream is no longer, and I am lucid—with full consciousness—eyes shut—as this remarkable, all embracing energy is exchanged between us—as if a dimensional alignment is achieved so that an energic 'totality' occurs. In this moment, I say instantly, knowing that it is he, 'I love you, Wilbur.' There is no fear, just complete openness to what is happening. The energy surge/correspondence lasts its full portion.

I am awed by its power and fullness, and so joyful that 'Wilbur' had made it across to me from the 'other side.' I know, in this moment, that he is aware that he has gotten through to me, and knows that I know it!

A 'coda' [to the visit] then arises, in which I am walking down a path—with stones in it—a woodland path leading away from the house. I am with this woman whom I am either following down the path or perhaps she is following me. As I travel the path, everything along it—all that grows—flowers, even plants, have 'faces' of personality—features which show them as conscious and sentient.

A ways down the path, the woman asks me, 'Do you have sight?' I know what she is asking me, and I respond, 'Yes.' She says, 'I'm starting/working to develop it.' I can tell that she doesn't really have it in the way that I now have it, but I smile at her as in a smile of gentle encouragement.

I then savor, fully awake as I lie in repose, this remarkable occurrence and experience, feeling, and sighing, a series of 'Wow's—quite filled with awe that this experience has found me.

I then decide to awaken Emily, who is asleep to my right, to let her know what has just happened.

Post 'dream,' I rest in sure knowledge of certain things.

Portion of the dream-log entry of Wilbur's visit, depict-
ing (however primitively) the "three ovals," along with the
description (referring to the topmost oval): "Wilbur's facial
features contained within this form," plus the following comment, "All three ovals, collectively, may have constituted—
been construed as constituting within the dream—Wilbur's
'energy body' or soul-energy." Note: At the point in the visitation reported in this portion of the dream log, the "energy"
has not yet been experienced as entering, or overlaying, the
neurology of the body of the dreamer. Hence the dream,
though vivid at this point, is not yet "lucid."

Part II
Commentary & Analysis

I

My first reaction following Wilbur's visitation was to just lie in bed, awake, in a state of rapture. The experience was beyond words, and I kept thinking, and even heard myself uttering repeatedly, in a low voice, "Wow . . . Wow . . . Wow . . . "

I decided to wake Emily up and let her know what had happened. Awakening Emily is not something I would ordinarily do, for she is very protective of her sleep, and doesn't fancy losing out on any. However, I did wake her. It was my first attempt to attach words to what had transpired, and my effort was halting and clumsy. She briefly wondered (we compared notes later) whether I might have gone a bit loopy, and be in need of transportation to McLean Hospital—the local nut-hatch. But I hadn't, and didn't; I felt as sane as I ever have (not that a protestation of sanity exactly slams the door shut on the possibility of madness).

Indeed, I felt rejuvenated, and wonderful! I realized that something major had transpired, and I was awash in savoring it. I also made an educated guess that the outflow from this experience would have far-reaching implications and long-term effects on my life—that it might, indeed, occupy me, on and off, for a number of years as I would periodically sidle up to it and mine it for more richness. Having this sense of the long-range consequences of such an experience arise in me so quickly, I lost any sense of urgency that I needed to be in a particular hurry to do anything with it. Its world and its deeper reckonings would await me at leisure.

For now I would revel—not too critically—in it. The experience was just so rich. There was a feeling of buoyancy that came into me. I was "light"—lightness. As earlier mentioned, I did not rush to write down the details of this visitation. The experience, even in my waking life over the following weeks and months, had very long tendrils. I don't want to overstate this, but the richness of savoring it was, in a way, part of the experience itself, and that richness—sheer delight, really—did not want to be boxed in by reductionistic "explanations" or "theories," or otherwise hemmed in by words. Unlike the usual experience in recalling dreams, in which a vivid recollection immediately following the occurrence of a dream seems to carry with it, in the moment, a convincing sense of permanence—only to, without any warning, quickly slip off the stage of consciousness and take flight into impenetrable gray mist—forever-after beyond retrieving—there was no fear of forgetting—no fear of details of *this* experience receding. It continued to be alive in me with considerable vividness, notwithstanding that, with the passage of time, I was gradually migrating to the "recollection" side of it.

It was at about the six-week point that I finally set down the definitive word-bound description, praying all the while that I could do it justice, both in fineness of detail and overall veracity. Once the written account existed, I didn't consult it again for over two years. However, my musings about the whole thing continued to playfully rock back and forth, to and fro, moving forward in my life along with me.

II

My first more serious reflections on Wilbur's visitation in the weeks and months following it were directed, primarily, to the manifest, or apparently obvious, elements of the experience itself.

At this manifest, obvious level I had had a subjectively "real" and compelling encounter with "Wilbur" nearly a year following his death. The encounter had faked me out, in that I hadn't been anticipating it, nor had I, beyond the pact that Wilbur and I had entered into in February of 2001, pursued it in any way. I hadn't even thought about it.

Also, in terms of the deal we had struck, Wilbur *hadn't* come to me I was out on the river. He hadn't intervened to keep me from venturing onto thin ice. This was April; daffodils were giving way to tulips amidst forsythia season. Ice was long-gone.

So, what sense could be made from this incongruity? Well, as I have previously noted, I knew at the time I did it that establishing my pact with Wilbur — the success of coming to an agreement — given Wilbur's disdain for all things holistic or loosey-goosey, would most likely be accomplished by framing the request for a post-death visit in terms that Wilbur would likely agree to — that of coming to the aid of a friend-in-need. It was possible, however — maybe all the more so if Wilbur had realized he was in possession of awareness post-death — that he would have figured out that the essence of the deal, at least from my end, hinged more on the question of whether or not consciousness extended beyond the grave. Against the weight of *that* question he presumably would have read-through the semi-ruse of the specific conditions I had stipulated in order to gain his cooperation. His post-death visit to me, then, would have still constituted his honoring of our agreement — the "spirit" of it, if not precisely the letter of it.

In any event: 1) Wilbur's consciousness had apparently survived bodily death, and 2) Wilbur had honored a commitment made before he died (though not exactly the "thin ice" part). Additionally, the energy forms that were first visible within the dream and then, as the dream turned lucid, actually (as I experienced it) entered my body and set up a resonance with it so that (the sense was) our neurologies (if I can all them this — it was neurology on my end, at least) were completely superimposed, overlaid, suffused, melded, concentrically aligned in that extraordinary, long (extended) interval, gave evidence of the amazing vibrancy — vitality — of whatever form Wilbur's being had assumed, or "gone home to," post-death. This vibrancy and robustness could not have been in starker contrast to the wasting physical form of Wilbur's diminished body as he lay dying from A.L.S.

III

Another early orientation in my initial perusal of, and reflection upon, these events had to do with the question of *how* to view them — through what lens, so to speak. I knew almost from the start that, to the extent I could attach a term of formalism to my efforts to make sense of these things and mine them for implications and meaning, it was important to stay grounded in the phenomenology, rather than strive to turn the whole thing into a metaphysical or religious treatise of some sort.

Indeed, most all religions find their foundation in the intensely personal and revelatory experience of their founder/prophet/messiah/enlightened one or the like. A compelling personal catharsis or epiphany leads to some sort of apotheosis in which that which is personal is extrapolated from to encompass all of humanity as a (sometimes, the!) proclaimed "chosen path." Even in the case of authentic humble origins, an elect—sometimes self-selected—group of followers seeks to lay claim to the experience of the founder as its own, and starts the inexorable process of establishing standards, rituals, taboos, the hierarchy of rank, time and grade, initiatory processes or sacraments, all of which are hung upon an expanding ganglia of organizational structure. Hence, a "religion" is formed.

However, Wilbur was an atheist, and I, for my part, am probably closer to being a heathen than to being religiously affiliated. This experience, for me personally, was not going to be summed up as the equivalent of Saul's conversion on the road to Damascus. Wilbur would never have stood for it. Nor am I evolved beyond the point where any such claim of personal transformation would simply constitute fart-food for the ego—mine, in this case. No. Whatever happened that night of Wilbur's visitation, whether fanciful, delusional, fictional or actual, was not going to be enshrined as the founding of any new movement, school, metaphysic or religion. Amen.

So where did that leave me in trying to fathom, and to mine, what *was* there? What about the phenomenology? Well, first, there was nothing about it that could ever be conclusively proved (or disproved, for that matter). Nor was there any lack of literature regarding accounts of post-death visitation—none of them any more provable than what I had experienced.

In the early twentieth century, for instance, the psychologist William James had made a pact with his dear friend and colleague Professor James Hyslop in which whoever pre-deceased would attempt to contact the other. James was the first to go, and apparently did manage to contact Hyslop via an Irish couple who fancied use of the planchette (ouija board). The apparently discarnate James employed a clever device that presumably would prove, to Hyslop, the authenticity of the communication and the identity of the communicator. James's "spirit," as channeled through the ouija board, posed the question, to Hyslop, as sent in the letter from the Irish couple: "Did you remember the red pajamas?" This question held specific meaning for Hyslop, for on a trip he and James had taken to Paris, their luggage had been misplaced, and in shopping to replace immediately needed items, Hyslop had purchased a pair of red pajamas. Hyslop reportedly felt that no one other than James would have known about them.[6] Notwithstanding the fact that Hyslop was quite convinced of the validity of this communication that circuitously reached him from the discarnate James, and took this occurrence as substantiation of the continuation of human consciousness beyond the grave, none of this, of course, proved a thing.

In the 1970s, Elizabeth Kübler-Ross's book, *On Death and Dying*, met with near universal acclaim as it dared venture into the area of dealing compassionately—and openly—with the issues of people who were confronted with the fact of dying—groundbreaking work in those days. Many years later, however, when Kübler-Ross dared to report that she had had apparitional en-

---

6) This anecdote is included in *Jung and The Story of Out Time*, by Laurens van der Post (see bibliography).

counters with the deceased, she was quickly marginalized as a figure who had gone loopy, and in pedigree (professional) circles, she and her career fell into disrepute.

Moving ahead to the 1990s, the psychiatrist Raymond Moody, whose earlier work had helped identify, and establish, in the early 1970s, the area of near-death experience as a legitimate field for respectful inquiry, became fascinated with the "Oracle of the Dead" of Greek antiquity and sought to solve its riddle: How did it work? As an experiment, he constructed a latter-day equivalent to the ancient psychomanteum, and reported (in *Reunions: Visionary Encounters with Departed Loved Ones*) some success in facilitating wakeful encounters with the deceased on the part of his patients. Again: anecdotally compelling, but nothing proven.

Interspersed with these three examples, spanning nearly a century, there were any number of books and case reports of post-death encounter—many evocative, yet all hopelessly inconclusive.

The risk of writing what is likely to be perceived as yet another book belonging to this aforementioned ilk is that it can be just as easily dismissed as an idiosyncratic, spurious account, "another one of those" (with the assessor's nostrils held and firmly pinched between the index finger and the thumb). However, since I really have no preceding reputation to defend or standing to maintain, I happily accept this risk, and choose to take it.

IV

A subjective experience always carries with it the conviction of constituting, for the person who has it, an objective reality. So here, lapsing into the subjective (which, after all, is always at the heart of personal experience, be it enthralling or scientifically dispassionate), is where I stand on this—where I find myself.

The experience of Wilbur's visitation is as subjectively "real" to me as any other experience I can recall, including the current experience of my sitting on a sunlit balcony on a delicious, easy Sunday in June, 2004, precisely at the noon hour (as I write "these words") writing this for you. So here, approached in a somewhat roundabout way, are some consequences for me personally that flow from this experience, now as I write this, over two years distant from that remarkable visitation.

There are many shades of "knowing" something. These include: "sure knowledge," "partial knowledge," belief, faith, intuition, conjecture, speculation, on down through hunch and superstition. As a result of the experience I have reported, my sphere of what I would consider "sure knowledge" has ratcheted up one notch—and one notch only. The one notch, or additional level, now appropriated as "sure knowledge" has a number of parts, but it can be boiled down to this: I have sure knowledge that consciousness—awareness—continues beyond what we refer to as bodily death (the apparent death of the person), and that this post-death consciousness contains elements that are recognizable as residues, or continuations, of aspects of the personal consciousness that was previously embodied. I now live with sure knowledge of this, notwithstanding the utter impossibility of ever proving any of it.

However, if I venture just one step beyond this level of "sure knowledge" into such questions as "What does it mean?" or "How is it set up?" I am *instantly* in the arena of speculation, belief, faith, hunch, and so on, along with just about everyone else. If I extrapolate from what I know "for sure," I venture into the realm of codifying a metaphysic or emplacing the tethering point for a faith or a creed. In other words, one step beyond what I "know," I am in the "partial knowledge" or "speculative knowledge" soup once again, with all attendant hazards.

It is not that I am unwilling to speculate or conjecture. (I shall do so presently.) It's that I'm not willing to proclaim anything on the basis of my speculations and conjectures, grounded as they are in the minimally augmented sphere of what I regard as "sure knowledge."

V

Regardless of the unprovability of certain kinds of phenomena, or the inherently subjective ground of all experience—including those carrying the hallmarks of "evaluation" and "rational," objective detachment—it may nevertheless prove illuminating to note what has been left in their wake. Quite possibly, given the fruits of a particular experience—what its "yield" is—it can be safely inferred that "something" happened. With this in mind, I need to report that post Wilbur's visit, I have noticed a couple of shifts in myself. These developments cannot yet be regarded as a long-term outcomes (though they may turn out to be). After all, Wilbur is only three-plus years departed, and his visit to me only happened, as of this writing, about two and a half years ago, so it is premature to take this report as bearing evidence of a profound transformation carrying forward over the duration of my remaining lifetime.

Nevertheless, here's what I can report: First, I appear to have lost my fear of death. This is not to say that I have lost my fear of *dying*. The process of dying, from what I have seen (in Wilbur and a number of others), is not a picnic. Encroaching—and then cascading—decrepitude, with its attendant adventures (and misadventures), does not look like much fun. I do not, as of now, look forward to this part of getting ready to depart. However, somewhere along the line in these occurrences involving Wilbur, I appear to have lost my fear of the apparently "final" outcome: death.

This surprises me, in a way, for many years ago, back in 1967, I knew someone, a lovely woman, who died, in her prime, as a result of a mishap while sky-diving. She was a wonderful person, a gentle soul with, proverbially, everything to live for. We were not lovers—more a reflection of her sound judgment than mine. But we were friends, and used to take drives together out into the countryside west of Boston. I hadn't seen her for a number of months, and then one day I heard of her death in a news broadcast on the radio.

Six months following her death I was messing around with a ouija board (sold as a child's toy or parlor game in those days) with someone I didn't know at all as my consulting partner sitting across the board from me. (This was an activity I hadn't seriously engaged in before. In hindsight, I realize that there is always a certain willfulness untempered by humility in any such meddling.) Without posing any question to the "board," the planchette just, all of a sudden, spelled out the name of my deceased friend. A brief "conversation," as mediated through the ouija board, appeared to ensue, in which it was developed that my deceased friend was "unhappy" on the "other side." My first reaction to this apparent break-through was complete, immediate, adrenal, egoistic exhilaration at having apparently pierced the veil—bridged the divide between life and death. My second reaction, following hot and heavy on the heels of the first, was . . . terror. Because the apparent encounter—though quite modest—was so unexpected, the magnitude of both the attendant euphoria and terror was extremely powerful and upsetting.

And terror won out! I went to see a friend—an older man whom I knew worked with children as a school counselor. I was quite distraught as I mentioned this experience to him. His "therapy" for me, impromptu, was to construct, ad hoc, a ouija board, and use it with me (while clearly evincing a highly skeptical attitude). Nothing "came through" the board. I was relieved, even though I couldn't get the thought out of my mind that his attitude was serving to sabotage the attempt. He then followed up on this demonstration by filling my deranged little noggin with enough psychological theory-on-the-run so as to reasonably convince me (believe me, I *wanted* to be convinced!) that the experience I had had earlier that day was of my own contrivance. "I" had moved the planchette because, as my more informed friend said, unbeknownst to me, "issues" about my relationship with Dede were residing in my "subconscious." The experience, which had brought me to the heights of euphoria collapsing into a morass of terror, was reduced, rationally, to a "mechanism"—and I was a complete and eager consumer of this explanation; it was a life raft to which I clung to avoid being pulled under into madness.

This experience of so long ago (I was twenty-one at the time) is salient in highlighting the other shift that has occurred within me since Wilbur's post-death visit: my apparently profoundly changed attitude regarding (a) the possibility of there being "life — existence — (consciousness) after death," and (b) my capacity to have compelling experiences that might point to this reality without personally freaking out.

I can offer one possible explanation for the evolution of this change. When I was twenty-one, I was drinking heavily, and my personal conduct and ethics mimicked the old Schlitz beer commercial of that time, the slogan of which was "You only go 'round once in life; you have to grab for all the 'gusto' you can!" My life, writ small, was dedicated to wholesale indulgence and the pursuit of instant gratification as the sole end and aim of corporeal existence. Youth, meaning indulgence and profligacy, was "forever," beyond which there was *nothing* (and no need for anything). In other words, a lifestyle geared to indulgence, instant gratification and self-destructive behavior could only "make sense" if the end were *really* the end — if there were no life after death.

Even a breath of the possibility of a continuation of anything beyond was enough to unleash a clash between how I was actually living, and what might confront me, in the long run, as a result. In short, my initial euphoria to the contrary, I was *not* eager to have *any* experience that would be suggestive of there being a continuation of consciousness beyond the grave. I probably, if asked prior to this experience, would have said I hoped for such a possibility. However this was "hoping" in the abstract. If there was a grain of reality to it, I didn't want it anywhere near me. I'm guessing that this attitude, forged on the foundation of a certain amount of shame, guilt and embarrassment over how I was living, is perhaps quite prevalent. Many, many people who claim a "belief" in an afterlife in the abstract, I suspect, wouldn't want to encounter evidence in support of it "up close and real personal." Just a hunch.

Within my friendship with Wilbur, however, my situation, over the intervening thirty-plus years, had become different. There was no fear, regret, destructiveness, remorse or guilt between us. There had been nothing unfinished (at least in worldly terms). Also, my life had gradually cleaned up — not to a level of sainthood, to be sure — but at least to the point of my being relatively comfortable living in my own skin. I was no longer leading a life geared to ceaseless repetition of pointless acts, as compounded by the wounding of others and the taking of reckless risks with my own life.

Therefore, I had less reason to fear the possibility that life, or consciousness of some sort, were it to exist after death, could lead to an indicting confrontation between me — with my espoused values — and my destructive behavior and its consequences. A perusal of my personal history now reveals to me that slowly — indiscernibly — I had become more open-ended regarding the possibility that death was not the final exit, and, in some strange way I don't even begin to understand, more available to the possibility of having some encounter with this reality whilst still on "this side" of things.

This is my best guess, in hindsight, of what had happened to me to liberate me from a crippling fear, and unblocked my availability to experience something unexpected. The complete and utter freedom from fear and terror that accompanied Wilbur's visit to me was a significant marker — an indication that my capacity to tolerate this kind of experience has come a very long way indeed.

Furthermore, this liberation from terror (as I have said, probably the last development I would *ever* have predicted for myself) was almost as significant to me as the experience of the actual visitation itself. And, of course, in my case the latter could not have happened without the former. To recap: that terror unleashed from that deserved ouija board jolt all those years before felt "burned in" to my neurology. I would have placed bets that it would always have me on the ropes. Therefore, as an epiphenomenon of my post-death encounter with Wilbur, it is with some satisfaction that I realize it is there no longer.

On balance, it strikes me that the alleviation of my fear of death, and the realization that I have the capacity to tolerate an experience of post-death visitation without sinking into a psychosis, are not inconsiderable outflows stemming from Wilbur's post-death visitation to me.

VI

I wish now to venture into the realm of inference and speculation as predicated on an assumption (for the purpose of this discussion) that Wilbur's post-death visitation of me was "actual"—something that, despite its unprovability, really happened.

The fact that "Wilbur," in whatever form he or his consciousness found themselves post-death, was able to make, successfully, the effort to get through to me suggests several things:

A. That there is a continuation, beyond death, of personal consciousness—at the very least a remnant of the prior, embodied consciousness—containing residues of the experiences encountered while "alive." In Wilbur's case, as suggested by the visible (within the dream) energy ovals (the sighting of which immediately preceded the dream's becoming lucid), there was a representation of Wilbur's "facial" features—not the face outright, but certain features which were highly identifiable within one of the energy ovals of the initial sighting. To take the image as emblematic, it appeared that the personal consciousness that was "Wilbur" in this life had re-coalesced with the larger overall—oval—energy form, though the personal consciousness continued to exist within the larger consciousness with particularities that were recognizable as "his."

B. *That there is the ability of post-death consciousness to retain awareness of, and, in certain instances, even to honor, commitments made with embodied individuals (persons). Such obligations, promises, commitments or agreements can be honored by the deceased from the vantage point of being post-death, with individuals who are still living (embodied) with whom these promises or commitments were made while the deceased person was still "alive."*

C. *That, on some level, embodied, time-bound life must be accorded some measure of meaning, importance, significance, value—I'm struggling to find the right word here—as assessed from other planes of existence or consciousness, that such commitments as might be made between someone soon to die and someone yet to live longer would be deemed worthy of being honored. In other words, embodied existence, as we know it, has an independently affirmed relevance, worth and importance. It is somehow meaningful and desirable, under certain* circumstances, that embodied, time-bound consciousness "here," be reached by unembodied (or other-bodied), out-of-time consciousness "there."

D. That, in the universal economy of what is possible (expendable?) and what is not (prohibited?), at whatever level such determinations are put in play, such contact is deemed possible, and "permitted." This line of reasoning suggests that beyond those occasions of there being post-death disembodied consciousness which has a desire to make good on an intention formed while "embodied," that the "Universe," regardless of whether this is conceived of in personified terms, or as an outworking of intrinsic laws and properties, actually permits, or allows for, this kind of wish or obligation to be realized or accomplished from the post-death situation.

E. That the ties of love, established during embodied life, carry beyond what we call death. In the limited case of Wilbur's and my relationship and his subsequent post-death visitation, this was certainly the case. Wilbur and I had a loving, abiding friendship, and it was the love held by this friendship that set the stage for what could develop within it, over the years, including the post-death deal that was honored. In some sense this platonic love, free of angst, irresolution, regret, guilt, second-guessing, and so on, created a very clear, pristine backdrop against which the post-death experience could unfold.

This is not to say that other obligations of soul that are other than "love-based" may not also carry-over and play out in some fashion, or that relationships with love in them, but also compounded by other amalgams—conflictual feelings, motivations and the like—may not also find post-death correspondence, but it is fair to speculate that in such cases post-death phenomenology, while perhaps still possible, would likely be more complex, even ambivalent, and therefore, as emotionally more loaded, all the more heavily resisted by those who, as still embodied, could be the recipients of visitations by those of the more problematic departed. Indeed, it would be understandable for people still "living" to have an unconscious aversion to post-death encounter if such an experience might include elements that were not necessarily "loving."

In consideration of the above, it would appear that the ties of love, as relatively uncompounded by irresolution or angst, would make the embodied consciousness's encounter with post-death phenomenology seem less threatening, and therefore more likely. Whether, in the cosmic scheme of things, it is the love-basis itself that actually creates the likelihood of post-death phenomenology *a priori*, or whether post-death phenomenology is a given of consciousness—part of our human capacity—and uncomplicated love merely fosters an attitude that makes one more inherently receptive (less resistant) to the realization and activation of our generic capacity for post-death contact, I haven't a clue.

In my own case, I suspect that if post-death confrontation with Wilbur had necessitated the weathering of strong conflictual emotions that stemmed from our earthly relationship, I doubt very seriously that I could have been open to the experience, and would probably have found, consciously and unconsciously, any number of means to sabotage or abort it. Indeed, the freak-out over that earlier ouija board experience, involving feelings of irresolution towards the deceased as compounded by a certain pervasive guilt of my own over how I was, overall, living my life, certainly suggests the complex range of responses that such an encounter would hold for those emotionally unprepared for them.

I am utterly grateful that Wilbur's and my relationship, as an uncomplicated love-based friendship, apparently paved the way for my being able to show up fully for the post-death encounter, and have, as I have said, no secondary reactions of fear and terror encumbering it, or scuttling it. The fact that "love abides," and can be honored beyond the grave, is a part of "sure knowledge" for me.

VII

I want to mention something about the "pathway" through which I was reachable, and "reached."

In general terms, the question of pathway is very important. For instance, if "Wilbur" had come to me in a dream (which, indeed is how my experience of his visitation started), and the dream had not become "lucid," then in recollecting the event, I would have been left with the impression that "Wilbur came to me in my dream," or "I had a dream about Wilbur last night."

These kinds of dreams are not at all uncommon; most people have had dreams of someone they knew who has died. If recalled, these dreams sometimes can bring much comfort. However, the impression necessarily remains: "I *dreamt* that . . ." The dream is the common ground for such encounters—neutral territory, perhaps—and remains the common feature of them. In meeting on "common ground," one does not become lucid, and the dream remains "a dream."

With lucidity, however, the main features are that one is wide awake (everyday wakeful consciousness) and, because the encounter involves this neurology—this pathway of everyday awareness—*the "energy" from the "other side" is experienced as having intentionally crossed the divide to extend into the embodied person's sensorium, his world, to reach him.*

The prevailing sense of such an experience is not that "I dreamt of X," but that "X came to visit me," or "X was here with me"—an altogether more vivid, compelling experience.

In my case it seems that the possibility that embodied human consciousness could knowingly, in full possession of its faculties, have experiences of a transcending, boundaries-breaching, domain-bridging nature was brought home to me by the pathway of lucid dreams, and the neurology invoked to support them—the neurological arrangment most commonly associated with chills, goose-bumps, energy rushes, "body slams" and the like.[7]

The onset of lucid dreams when I was about thirty-three years old was, as previously elaborated, unanticipated. This range of experience was, to the best of my knowledge and recollection, utterly unknown to me prior to this time. Yet, beyond holding a certain fascination for me as one of consciousness's flexations, lucid dreams had never revealed themselves to me as holding a *personal* meaning or purpose for *me*—that is, until "Wilbur" showed up. Wilbur's visit was the first instance, in over twenty years of sporadic recurrence, in which this kind of dream seemed "used" for something particularly specific, purposeful and personally meaningful. My neurology—that involved to support,

---

7) These speculations and musings follow upon an essay entitled: "Goosebumps, Shivers and 'Body Slams': Embodying Consciousness's Exaltations," which comprises Chapter 8 in my book *Who's at Home in Your Body (When You're Not)? Musings on Consciousness by a Participant-Observer* (publication pending). The manuscript for this book was written in 1998 or so, three years before Wilbur's death, and indeed before there was even any obvious indication that he was soon to face terminal illness.

in the body, a "lucid" experience while dreaming—was, as I experienced it, specifically harnessed in furtherance of an agenda sourced beyond my neurology's alignment at the time of the visitation. This was the pathway that had been inaugurated all those years before, and finally, extending for the moment beyond the conundrum of what it was all about, was set into service to fulfill a decidedly transcendent, meaningful purpose that was personally relevant.

This energy from the dream, as the dream became lucid, had cascaded into the alignment of my body's neurology—that more usually experienced (at a much more attenuated level) with body chills (including chills running up and down the spine, goose-bumps, energy surges and "pins-and-needles" sensations, and so on). This embodied pathway was, at the height of Wilbur's visit, about (as best I can gauge it quantitatively) 20 times stronger, more engulfing, intense and pervasive than the more usual "chills-up-and-down-the-spine" occurrence that many people would experience in a situation, say, of feeling deeply "moved" by an encounter with something aesthetically beautiful or awe-inspiring.

In the actual merging of energies that occurred at the height of Wilbur's visit, the energy surges spread throughout my whole body in a rapid, heightening succession of waves, the trough between each of which was deeper and deeper than the one preceding, leading to a final, extended moment of sustained energy superimposition.

This description makes the experience sound orgasmic, but sexual or sensuous faculties were not a part of it. There was no "orgasm" in the pedestrian sense. It was all "energy"—energy as a pervasive, resonant vibrancy involving what I experienced as the closest correspondence between two life-forms: one we would call embodied, and the other we might term disembodied or "differently-bodied."

I do need to report that the lucid experience of merging, energetically, with another life form had occurred in two lucid dreams over the preceding score of years. In one, I was leaping from one rock outcropping to another, along with a panther who was also leaping in tandem with me. With the leap into the air (similar to becoming airborne in other lucid dreams), lucidity occurred, and at the moment of lucidness the panther and I merged, mid-air—as each of us was fully extended and committed to the leap—into one another in a precise superimposing of our energies. The "body slam" (energy rush) experience developed simultaneously with the superimposition, and then the dream image quickly faded though my lucidity/conscious awareness continued, unbroken. On another occasion (in 1993) I had a similar lucid dream in which a large, diaphanous dragonfly with a dancing play of iridescence entered, at the moment of lucidity, my head and somehow, energetically, overlaid me. This again fired off the "chills" neurology. At the time of the occurrence of each of these lucid dreams, they seemed to underscore a singular capacity of the body's neurology to link with the energy of lucidity and somehow "ground" it in the body, lending lucidity a convincing quality of being "embodied."

However, as with the case with lucidity generally, the two earlier experiences with merger-"chills" in the context of lucid dreams did not carry a personal meaning or relevance to me until that neurology was invoked to be both the pathway and the means through which Wilbur's visit would become grounded as a bodily reality to me.

113

VIII

What I have heretofore described is the sequence of occurrences over a period of twenty-plus years that appears to have led to the fashioning of a neurological arrangement through which "I" could be "reached" by experiences of alternate realities or possibilities while functioning, myself, in a state of everyday, wakeful consciousness (and still embodied!).

Yet, it would be a mistake to take the neurological arrangement that seems to have evolved for me to be the sine qua non of preparation for transcendent experiences. In truth, regarding whatever skill or talents I may possess about such matters, I have never felt particularly gifted along these lines. I am not, as far as I know, "psychic" or "clairvoyant" in any sense of the word. Though a meditator for many years, my practice is fairly self-styled. All these years later it remains personally helpful to me in staving off high blood pressure, and in furthering my emotional balance (such as it is), especially in the course of meeting life's challenges on a daily basis (and I'm not aware that life has necessarily treated me particularly gently in this respect). It has never, however, provided an obvious, direct portal to transcendent experience, although it is possible that neurological rearrangements, as incremental epiphenomena within meditation, may tweak the body's neurology in this direction.

I actually got involved with meditation many years ago, in the mid-1970s, long before any lucid dreams had started to show up (consistent with the possibility that meditation may pave the way for such occurrence). As mentioned, I had had occasion to use meditation as a means of countering high blood pressure, which had been diagnosed in me by the ripe old age of thirty. I was providentially placed in touch with Herbert Benson, M.D.'s

The Relaxation Response (in which Dr. Benson studied the physiological effects of Transcendental Meditation and realized their relevance to the treatment of hypertension and stress), and had quickly adapted for my own use the generic techniques for meditation presented in his book. I had experienced a euphoric reaction early on as my body's own stress-clearing capability was evoked. My high-blood pressure was "history" within about a week; over the past 27 years (as I write this) it has never returned, and as I have said, life has not necessarily been, in the meantime, any kinder to me or less stressful than it is to most people. Although the euphoric initial reaction to meditative practice subsided quite quickly, the medical/health benefits did not. I have been a daily meditator ever since.

A couple of decades later, I taught meditation classes for several years at a couple of health and fitness clubs—kind of a moonlighting activity. I continued to encounter a number of reticent students who, though initially enthusiastic about exploring meditation, had felt stymied in prior attempts to "learn" meditation because, as was clear to me, the type of meditation they had been exposed to was not a match for how they were neurologically configured, at least at the outset.

As a teacher of meditation, I would have considerable success in helping such students discover that they were capable meditators, and here's how I could do it: Through my own explorations and adaptations, I had come to appreciate that *any* of the sensory pathways can be the "road in" to developing a wonderful, rewarding meditative practice. The error in so much meditation teaching is to attempt to impart a method that is too narrow or confining to be useful to students with differently constituted neurology. Good meditation teaching needed to introduce would-be meditators to a *range* of styles, techniques and options, so that each student could discover his/her own pathway — the sensory function(s), be it sight, hearing, the olfactory, touch, proprioception, taste, sensing, or intuition — that, either individually or in some combination, would work for him/her. Indeed, experience had taught me that *any* single one of the sensory faculties could become a highway into meditative experience and adventure.

In my case, the body-centered "sensory" and "proprioceptive" capacities had revealed themselves as my strong suits. (As a "visualizer," I was as inert as a lead pipe!) However, others came to have equally compelling and meaningful meditative experiences involving neurological arrangements of sensory faculties that were (and still are) completely alien to my experience.

So . . . possible lessons to be derived from this little exposé on "becoming reachable," and meditation are:

1. It is possible that a meditative practice may lead, cumulatively, to a gradual refinement of a person's neurology rendering him or her a possible candidate for transpersonal occurrences. This is not to say that meditation should be undertaken with the intention of cultivating this outcome[8], only that a refined neurology, as an evolving artifact of meditation, may increase the likelihood of the occurrence of such experiences as an epiphenomenon of meditation.

2. Perhaps more importantly, meditation may lead a practitioner, as s/he develops an awareness of what "works" for him/her in meditation — which of the sensory capacities

---

8) The question of whether it is advisable to knowingly pursue transcendent experiences as a goal in itself is addressed in the following section.

come into the foreground as pathways into it — to a recognition of how s/he may be "reachable," and "reached," by transcendent events.

And so, while I have considerable familiarity with how my neurology aligns in ways that make me "reachable," how it is for me is less compelling than the apparent fact that *each person can discover and become, over time, more open to the specific pathway(s) which render him/her "reachable."* In the overall scheme of things, no one pathway, whether "visual" or "non-visual," is necessarily any better than any other. The only thing that matters is individual capacity and preference. One doesn't "imitate a technique"; rather, one discovers "what works for oneself."

So, to summarize: These experiences in meditation, and what I have derived from them, would seem to indicate that it is possible to discover the specific pathways through which a given person is "reachable" regarding transcendent experiences, including those possibly involving post-death encounter. These pathways would seem to develop along any of the sensory faculties a person discovers him/herself to have operative during meditation. It is suggested that these pathways possibly develop, over time, regardless of any conscious intention on the part of the meditator to develop them.

IX

Conscious intention. Hmmmm. Does conscious intention have a role here? Should one knowingly endeavor to develop such capacities — a way to bridge the corporeal and the ineffable?

Well, this much I can offer. As I have said, it seems clear, if there is any validity to the experience I had with Wilbur's post-death visitation with me, that an importance exists regarding how bodily/earthly/corporeal life is regarded, that there be *any* effort made at all, on the part of other (apparently) disembodied consciousnesses and their energies, to inform our limited, embodied selves, *while* embodied and so limited, with overtones of a more extensive, transcendent reality. Indeed, my experience suggests that effort—energy—must be expended, or made available, from "the other side," to accomplish this. "Getting through," even under the most aligned of circumstances, is an effortful act, and therefore presumably linked with an intention, on the part of "other" consciousness, to do so. In other words, it takes work—exertion—hence, we may surmise, a determination from *that* direction has to have been made that the expenditure of effort is, for whatever purpose, *worth* making.

However, does the existence (if true) of an intention from the "other side" to reach us necessarily oblige us to develop ourselves with the intention, from "our side," of becoming available to being "reached," and capable of tolerating such experiences? My considered opinion on this key question is: "Not necessarily." For one thing, these experiences can be decidedly upsetting, even frightening and terrifying, if one is not well prepared for them. As I have mentioned several times to this point, I never thought that I would ever surmount the terror I encountered during that ouija board flirtation all those years ago. It has been well said that "The psychotic drowns in the same ocean where the mystic swims in delight." I *know* what it feels like to be in fear of my own sanity—either the terror that I'm losing it (and slipping over the edge), or that I have to actually live *within* it!—that I *am* aware, and the reality which I'm obliged to acknowledge, and see through sane eyes, is horribly upsetting. These kinds of experiences are not easy to endure. I honestly don't know how I've come through some of them—especially the earlier ones.

Speaking only in personal terms, if my overall experience has anything to contribute to the question of *intentionally* attempting to pursue transcendent possibility, it may go something like this. (Please feel free to extrapolate from these points in any way that suits you.)

Admittedly, my behavior, both what I have written about and related in this account (and much that I haven't mentioned), reveals that I have had a longstanding fascination with death, and that this fascination, at some level, has been operative in me for a very long time (although I haven't always been conscious of my preoccupation). The whole exercise of ice skating on a river in the dead of winter is metaphorically all about death—arguably an elemental displacement of my intrinsic preoccupation. One skates on a membrane of ice. On one side is life as I know it; on the other, should I fall through, is drowning (in water—one of the most ubiquitous symbols of the unconscious), or "life on the other side." So there is this fascination that, arguably, has always been with me—is part of how I'm made—and comprises a principle of my being.

However, despite my life-long fascination (which, in my case, took, at the outset, more the forms both of counter-phobic daredevil derring-do, and the conjurings of a meddling sorcerer's apprentice who runs the risk of getting carried away under the spell of enticement as compounded by lack of knowledge and experience), I was, in my earlier years, truly not "ready to know." My curiosity was a gadfly, but my capacities were not recognized, let alone awakened. My life was disorderly and unruly, and my mental, emotional and spiritual constitution was fragile.

Yet, unbeknownst to me, my "talents"—and I use the word very loosely here—were starting to develop. Off alcohol and other substances by age twenty-four, followed by many years of cleaning up my own mess (or, to be fair, at least creating fewer messes, as I plodded along in life, than I was managing to clean up), during which I was, as mentioned, introduced to meditation as a specific means to address hypertension (and through most of which, I should add, I was developing my on-ice friendship with Wilbur), my neurology was continuing to "shake-down and line-up."

Those initial lucid dreams, arriving at a point when, in hindsight, I realize that I was already a number of years along in this process, were likely epiphanous of the neurological milestones that were being reached, and the ranges of experience that were starting to become accessible to me—*or, more likely, to which I was becoming accessible*—as a result. So without "intending to," developments were ongoing behind the scenes, and conscious clues, however enigmatic, were starting to reach me.

Had I set out willfully to find such experience—to develop my capacities with the intention of pursuing the transcendent—I think I would have run certain risks. I'm guessing that these risks exist for most, if not all, unsuspecting (and therefore vulnerable) "seekers" across the board. Here I shall outline and expand on some of them.

The first risk stemming from willfully pursuing the transcendent is that I could have encountered negative transpersonal experiences that would have been deeply disturbing at the least, and sanity-threatening at the worst. Indeed, I did have a brush with this kind of consequence during that ouija board fiasco I let myself blunder into much earlier in life. My own extreme reaction to a possible, earlier post-death encounter with a person with whom the relationship—even though neither "love-based," physically intimate nor hostile—nevertheless carried conflictual elements, was complicated and problematic. This reaction, I suspect, may typify what one can expect from certain post-death encounters. Such encounters would, understandably, taint the whole phenomenon of post-death contact as a range of experience to be categorically cast off as undesirable.

A second risk I could have been faced with concerns the category of post-death encounter with individuals with whom I had been involved, at some point during their embodied life, in a relationship of "love-based" intimacy. As I believe that these risks I'm outlining are generic ones, I want to comment on this point, and those to follow, in more general (and therefore less personal) terms. For the purpose of this discussion, I'll address relationships of "love-based intimacy" as a class—a group unto itself—that holds potential for post-death encounter.

So what about them—these relationships that are decidedly "love-based?" Can they qualify as suitable candidates for post-death encounter? And . . . are there any particular risks that pertain to post-death encounters with individuals who fall into the "intimate, love-based" category?

God knows, physically intimate love-based relationships could, it would seem, certainly serve as vehicles for this kind of experience. The fact that such relationships often have, as features within them, considerable trust, teamwork and shared life experience would seem to make them a "natural" as candidates for post-death encounter.

However, it is only fair to point out that in the more intimate, sexualized, "partnering" relationships there is *still* likely — maybe even *especially* likely — to be a certain amount of ambivalence, along with "issues" seeking resolution — which does *not* mean that these relationships are not loving, but, rather, that there is (and perhaps always is in any such relationship) deeper conflict, and even a portion of bitterness, as a part of the mix.

In fact, the general level of co-dependency and intensity intrinsic to intimate relationships that are *neurotically* based — in extreme, more enmeshed cases the agony/ecstasy, bliss/desperation, "roses and razorblades" combo — would presumably constitute a large part of the draw — the motivation — for willfully pursuing the development of one's own transcendent abilities following the death of someone with whom we had been intimately involved, however healthily or unhealthily, while s/he was alive (even as these attributes likely accounted for, in a largely unconscious way, the initial attraction in coming together while embodied).

This attraction to post-death meddling is understandable. It can prove hard not to want to wade into personal drama and narrative — to expiate an ancient guilt; to make someone, with finality, "truly understand"; to achieve some culminating sense of closure or, in the more neurotically impaired, to attempt to make someone yield to one's own willful desires and priorities; or to trump via vindictive triumph — utilizing *whatever* planes of influence that may become available, or developable. In such instances, Divine — or Universal — intention can often get blotted out by the pounding, throbbing imperatives-of-the-moment of local, imperious, personal needs, wants and desires.

Hence, the presence of the negative side of this ambivalence — of emotional conflict, irresolution, guilt, bitterness and the like — combined with a goodly dose of self-will, while not necessarily thwarting the possibility of post-death encounter, would likely inject themselves into any experience of this sort, coloring it in ways that might not be comforting, and could even be quite disturbing, notwithstanding the allure and seductiveness of attempting to establish post-death contact.

By way of contrast, I'm quite convinced that the success of having the experience I had with Wilbur, as I have alluded earlier, could only, in my case, have been realized via a relationship that was love-based and *non*-conflictual — in this case, an unconflicted, love-based *friendship*. This fact alone precluded my being "at risk" for encountering anything of a negative or wayward nature coming across the divide to harrass me.

I touch base, once again, with these observations in the interests of presenting the following possibility: Perhaps the best way (if one is truly intent on doing so) to train or prepare oneself for possible post-death encounter of the *positive* variety (regardless of whether one is embodied or disembodied) is to cultivate loving friendship as an ideal. This quality of relationship may be what truly prepares the way for subsequent heart-based developments. I suspect that the cultivation of this objective may be more conducive to the eventual possibility of experiencing uplifting post-death visitation than any willful pursuit of "techniques" regarding meditation, or other course of study with the intention of somehow creating, controlling, manipulating or otherwise "forcing" or managing such experiences.

This does not mean that meditation or yoga or other "alternative" approaches and regimens are not useful in developing a spiritual path, and in realizing emotional balance and greater compassion while developing increasing discernment. However, the point may be that in utilizing and developing "practices" or "devotions," one should not be too demanding or goal-specific. Open-ended easefulness may be better. On balance (not that it's exactly an "either/or" situation) I suspect that, concerning post-death encounter, cultivating relationships of "loving friendship" is probably more of a factor in the safe realization of transpersonal possibilities than any other facet of "training of mind."

The third risk of willful pursuit of the transcendent may seem paradoxical, but partially stems from the first two.

If in the first risk there is the possibility of inadvertently courting uncomfortable encounters and even sanity-threatening occurrences, and if the second risk brings with it the recognition that even love-based, physically intimate relationships can carry within them problematic elements that could work against the possibility that post-death encounters would necessarily be uplifting, the third risk is that, just as sometimes happens in corporeal life, we may feel impelled to "get involved"—and get sucked in (suckered in?)—by the very intensity generated in any number of relationships that are *not* necessarily love-based, and may even be primarily abusive and exploitive, rather than have the presence of mind to conduct a clear-headed appraisal as to whether or not wading into a situation of this sort is actually good for us, or otherwise warranted in any way.

Furthermore, as far as I know, we all have, in one form or another, "loaded"—emotionally charged—relationships in our past that carry amalgams of hopes and fears, expectations and disillusionments, visions and dreams-dashed, trusts and betrayals (trusts and trysts?), dependency and abandonment, bliss and ugliness. We carry this charge in the form of mnemonic residue. This energy residue is a living reality within us, even if we're not aware of it, *and* it can leave us with a certain susceptibility. If the transcendent possibility is a generic attribute of human consciousness—a faculty, so to speak—then it naturally follows that, if we are indiscriminately open to whatever is "there," then whatever "comes across" the divide to meet us—seductive or otherwise—is potentially whatever *is there* to come across—including that which could be attracted by our unsuspected vulnerability.

Such a vulnerability involves a person's being in a state that is highly impressionable, and therefore very open to being influenced or manipulated. If the transcendent pathway is a generic capacity of human consciousness, then it naturally follows that such a pathway may function primarily as a conveyer, and *not* necessarily as a filter. Just as I have discovered the painful, though necessary life lesson (while embodied) that not everyone on this side—the "earthly" side—of the pale necessarily holds my best interests at heart, so, too, this discordant challenge is plausibly the case with some energies emanating from the "other side" as well, especially if one is uncritically open to "being in the way" of them, or otherwise unknowingly attracts them.

Paradoxically, all the angst and sense of drama inherent in emotional conflict that contribute their zip to negative encounters (which, at first blush, would seem to make them candidates to be readily avoided) can also exert a kind of beguiling attraction that feels linked to fate, and can be *very* hard to resist. If relationships of this sort can sometimes be difficult to sidestep in our encounters with others in the course of our day-to-day lives, how much more so if they are alloyed with the whole notion of "establishing contact beyond the grave!" Indeed, it is possible that the whole notion of establishing "post-death" contact can exert a kind of seductive appeal that can blunt one's own discernment regarding just what (or whom) we may actually be getting (re)involved with. Self-will in playing with matches can, in such instances, lead to severely burned fingers.

A fourth pitfall that may await those who follow a rigorous practice of some sort with the objective of having post-death encounters—and "achieving" them, in this case—is that such attempts may all too easily be ego-driven, and any apparently successful experience of "contact" can easily lead to ego-inflation.

This is the "sorcerer's apprentice" kind of phenomenon in which one becomes drunk on one's own fancied abilities, not realizing how meager they may truly prove to be in the face of an unexpected tempest. This was the meddlesome influence that was so seductive and tempting to me at an earlier stage of life. Ego-inflation always involves the identification by the conscious will with its own goals and attainments. The apparent realization of a goal is taken to be a "personal" triumph, or break-through. This strong identification with apparent success is very intoxicating. Such an identification can lead to grandiosity and the cultivation of the further aim, as an end in itself, of holding influence and power over other people.

Indeed, there does exist in native cultures a whole tradition that combines transpersonal experiences with the directed will and ego-intention. This is the shamanic tradition. The shamanic literature is filled with accounts of "soul retrieval" and post-death encounters of various descriptions. The shaman him/herself is a powerful force in the community, often both feared and relied upon to enact spiritually based "healing" interventions involving journeys to the "other side." Spells, incantation, chants, high-velocity hypnotic drumming, rattling and dancing along with, in some (but certainly not all) cultures, the ingestion of psychoactive compounds, are employed as a means to effect altered states of consciousness, leading to the projection of consciousness into other (and otherworldly) planes of manifestation and experience. Notwithstanding the healing intentions, and accomplishments, of some (though not all) undertakings of this sort, personal will and willfulness are inextricably involved in these "directed" experiences, and within the shamanic tradition, reports of sha-manic "warfare" involving sometimes lethal, out-of-body battles over spheres of influence and power are not all that unusual. Transpersonal phenomena, within this tradition, are considered as the personal possession, or attainment, of one (the shaman) who develops it. It is equated with *personal* power.

If this ancient tradition, existing with remarkable consistency through millennia and across a range of cultures, has anything to offer us by way of helping us to become oriented towards trans-personal phenomenology in a "correct" way, it may boil down to something like this: Yes, it is possible to develop faculties or capacities that are ego-directed, and that may engender the occurrence of a range of transpersonal or transcending experiences — some of which may even be facilitative of certain kinds of healing. However, ego-directedness can attempt to appropri-ate such experiences as "personal" possessions or triumphs, and then egotism can really step in, vaunting and promoting its own "attainments" as something worthy of de facto veneration (in the form of "aspiring to") by the less attained. Cults and "guru-doms" are just one offshoot of such an unholy enterprise.

A personal identification with what may, in the final analysis, only be a "skill," potentially available to all, inevitably leads to proclamations of "the way" by those who feel they have found "it" (though, more likely, they have merely stumbled onto one version of "it").

Anyone, therefore, who identifies with such a "gift" as a "personal possession" (when in fact the person, in such an instance, is in a state of *actual* possession — "possessed" by the gift!) can only maintain influence as long as his "gift" is set apart as either inaccessible to others, or more developed than what is attainable by others. It follows that such a "leader" has influence only to the extent that s/he is playing off of the apparent deficiencies of other people. Often, at the root of it all is an agenda to foster in others an unhealthy dependence on oneself, tantamount to having a vested interest in *not* sharing — not helping other people develop the very capacities s/he holds in trust, and wields "as a public good."

By contrast, my own post-death encounter with Wilbur seemed to find me. As mentioned, it is obviously true that I have a fascination both with death and the unconscious, and to a certain extent, I have quested to know more — learning what I can along the way. However, beyond the formal reading I have done, and the meditation practice that developed over the years (which had, at the outset, a medical provenance, not a spiritual one), and despite an ignorance and immaturity that could have left me open, very early on, to abusing — and being abused by — any "powers" that might have come my way, the line-up of experiences, including arguably the whole relationship with Wilbur of thirty-plus years with its crucial ingredient of love-sans-conflict, and that early burst of lucid dreams that brought to me a recognition of conscious capacities I had not, knowingly, heretofore experienced—those elements, along with others—a river in winter, a white-haired elder on ice, and so on, taking shape as they did—*they all found me*. I could not have "willed" them, in the usual sense of the word.

So, somewhere, coursing through this welter of comments, caveats and observations, there exists the fine line between "willfully" cultivating a possibility, and "willingness"—maybe, especially a "*readiness*"—to be reached by, and *shown by*, a possibility. Perhaps what constitutes the correct balance between these disparate attitudes is a riddle for each person to resolve in his/her own way. I am grateful to have found my answer . . . and to that extent, it would seem that finding an answer is possible.

X

On a personal note, although there have been no subsequent visits from "Wilbur" (in whatever form his energy has assumed since that early morning on April 15th, 2002), the experience still seems open-ended to me. I don't really expect any further visitation from him. On a practical level, he more than honored the agreement we made prior to his bodily death. There is no promise remaining to be kept. I love him earnestly, and assume that "he" has gone on to whatever adventures as yet await "him" on some odyssey that is beyond my comprehension—and probably even beyond my capacity to comprehend.

However, *I* have the freedom—given the way that this experience, and all the prior happenstances that lined up to create it, reached me—to be open-ended as to where, if anywhere, this acquisition of a further increment of what I regard as "sure knowledge" will lead me. Not necessarily any less of an egoist than my fellow human brethren, I can just note that there is no sense of clinging, of having to extract some "return" or other from it, some yield as from an investment. It is true that I have felt an obligation to honor this experience by way of writing this book. However, the completion of this task has lifted from me whatever burden *that* responsibility held. Mission accomplished. The future, insofar as I am, for the moment, obliged to exist "in time," seems very open-ended to me regarding the ramifications of knowing something of post-death consciousness. My world, in deeply personal, intimate ways, has changed, and I am likely a better, more thoroughly human person for it.

Less the desire to clasp the experience and strangle or throttle it into some conformity, predictability or "yield," it is simply there, existing only as one of probably countless flexations of human consciousness, or perhaps of consciousness as a generic component of existence.

Rather than something I seize as some narrowly construed victory, Wilbur's post-death visit to me, and all that led up to it, washes over me as blessing upon blessing.

XI

To some extent, the meta-question perfusing the whole matter of the validity of an experience of post-death visitation relates to the old cognitive/philosophical quandary: "If a tree falls in the forest, and there is no one there to hear it, does it make a sound?" I would (as is my wont) emboss the question with this twist: "Is reality only what our senses and neurochemistry tell us it is (thereby internally generated by them)? . . . Or is reality—always and ever—extending on into the 'background,' beneath the radar of our awareness, ever shaping the origin of our experiences of reality in ways that our 'perceiving' can never know directly—ways that are beyond what is directly attributable to 'sense and neurochemistry?'" This question seems pertinent to me, notwithstanding its rhetorical nature.

In writing this account of my relationship with Wilbur and the post-death experience, I have tried to be objective in my reporting and assessment of these events. However, no amount of careful discernment can hold fast against the obvious: an admission that at heart such experiences are all subjective, and unprovable. As I have admitted elsewhere, I am aware that, given the literature that exists involving post-death encounter, it will be easy for anyone so inclined to dismiss this humble offering as just "another one of those . . ." I write this account and the commentary in full awareness that the reception this work will receive will likely include both hostility and ridicule.

It's OK with me. I don't write this book primarily for these folks, even though I hope some of them will actually read it, and dare to derive something useful from it. Additionally, I appreciate that Scientism is the current religion of the land—the secular religion of our age—and, typically, deems as unworthy of study any range of experience that is not subjectable to the scientific method, with its testable hypotheses, controlled variables and replicable findings, all leading to well-buttressed theory that generates subsequent hypotheses which are further testable by controlled experiments, and on and on.

The negative bias towards a spirit of serious inquiry regarding the "untestable" is often presented with an air of dispassionate objectivity. However, the bias itself, just as often, has an *emotional* underpinning more accurately characterizable as "contempt prior to investigation." This book will likely be assessed by numerous acolytes of Scientism as having nothing useful to offer. However, it is still written with them in mind, with the hope that they will read it. After all, Wilbur's viewpoint prior to the time of his dying was exactly this. I believe he would want anything purporting to present honestly a version of his experience to be open to all comers. Wilbur was always more generous of heart than I am.

XII

Along the course of my education I have come across a number of works involving heartening—and disquieting—reports of strange phenomena, not readily testable in the quantitative, scientific sense of the word—yet intriguing, nonetheless. These experiences imposed themselves on their subjects, and in each case the person to whom they occurred was, initially, in fear for his sanity, and highly doubtful as to the legitimacy, or "realness," of what he was being obliged to undergo.

The story in each of the writings and transcripts that eventually issued forth from these unwilling subjects is a story, to be sure, about the strange phenomena with which each, respectively, was confronted—and in each case, it is true, the veracity of the reported experiences themselves is open to legitimate question. *Yet the larger story, in each case, is the struggle each person went through in "entering into conscious relation" with whatever was happening, learning to fend off the degree of madness which seemed to threaten, and, ultimately, developing a kind of familiarity with the phenomenology based on involuntary participation combined with impressive powers of self-observation and scrutiny.* In each case a "mastery," of sorts, resulted, in which the person did, indeed, not go mad, and the experiences, after a fashion, became more normalized and, to some extent, harnessable or deployable for a purpose.

These individuals triumphed over the "gifts" that were imposed on them by acknowledging them rather than denying them, by avoiding overly identifying with them as personal "possessions," by managing not to become ego-inflated once a familiarity with their respective phenomenology had been won, and by remaining skeptical as to the full implications of what they had been through despite their mastery of the phenomenology. Their spirit of serious inquiry was sustained, and their sense of humility never left them. None of them left a "religion," as such, in his wake.

The first of these is Robert Monroe who, unbidden, was subjected to, initially, a series of terrifying out-of-body experiences (which arose from everyday wakeful states, rather than from transitions while sleeping) — this at a time (the 1960s) when a middle-class American businessman (and almost everyone else) would not have ever heard mention of "out-of-body experiences." *Journeys Out of the Body* is Monroe's account of how he reconnoitered these occurrences. It is an impressive account. His challenges, and the hard-fought mastery he achieved, are heroic in stature. His later volume, *Far Journeys*, builds on the first and gives insight into the evolving scope of Monroe's achievement many years down the road. I have few heroes, but Robert Monroe comes close to being one of them.

The next person who combines similar qualities is Whitley Streiber. The phenomenon that seized Streiber falls under the heading of what is termed "abduction experiences." Streiber was subjected to intrusive experiences of what might be termed "alien visitations." This category of phenomena has remained controversial, and much (though not all) of the "evidence" ostensibly corroborating such happenstances has been openly discredited. However, upon reading Streiber's book, *Communion*, one again is treated to an account of an intelligent, self-observant person who, *to his chagrin*, is obliged to fathom a range of happenings that are extremely disconcerting and upsetting. Streiber, in the interest of determining both for himself and as a statement of record for others whether he *was* or *was not* mentally ill, subjected himself to extensive psychological testing and psychiatric consultation. That he achieved some sense of normalizing for himself a range of these upheaving experiences, even as he managed to pass for "normal" in the everyday world in which he functioned is, again, a remarkable personal accomplishment. A sequel called *Transformation* offers, as in Monroe's case, a perspective on his experiences, as he continued to integrate them over a more extended time frame. Both Streiber and Monroe bear evidence of a capacity to be confronted with bizarre phenomena and, through an evolving discernment born of participant-observation, to successfully integrate their respective experience of alternate realities into the fabric of a whole life capable of interfacing well enough with society. Although the experiences to which each is subjected can, in and of themselves, be viewed as psychotic episodes, and even discounted as spurious fabrications, neither of these men is insane[9], either by virtue of having the experiences themselves, or in their adaptive "learning curve" response to them.

---

9) Bear in mind that "insane" is a legal term, not a psychological one.

A third person I would mention in this regard is Edgar Cayce. His situation was different in character and tone from either Monroe's or Streiber's. Monroe and Streiber were participant-observers in phenomena that confronted them. Cayce was not. As a trance-medium "he" was absent—his everyday wakeful consciousness had "broken off" from engagement with the outer world—while "channeling" psychic readings for others. His gifts of prophesy, accurate medical diagnosis, and prescription via psychic means (well documented) all came forth while "he"—the consciousness of the everyday "Edgar Cayce"—was vacant his body. He would be told of things "he" had said while in trance; however, he would have no memory of having said them.

Cayce, therefore, could only learn about his apparent channeling gifts second-hand, so to speak. Others who witnessed these phenomena and took notes on "his" utterances while "he" was in trance would have to tell him about these experiences—and what transpired within them while "he" was absent. Cayce was highly resistant to believing that he was gifted as a psychic channeler—a trance-medium. Indeed, while allowing himself, over a number of years, to submit to hundreds upon hundreds of trance-medium sessions (for which a written record exists), he remained skeptical, throughout his adult life, as to the validity of his apparent gift.

Neither Monroe, nor Streiber nor Cayce sought to establish a religion or cult based on the vantage point of their unusual experiences and the apparently enlarged scope of consciousness they were each afforded because of them. They remained "right-size." It is, however, true that in Cayce's work a kind of metaphysics involving reincarnational themes is adducible, and Monroe did start an institute with the intention of assisting others in developing their own capacities for having out-of-body experiences. Also, in Monroe's work there is phenomenology that is reported which is consistent with experiences of post-death encounter. However, not one of them sought to capitalize on his respective gifts in a way that could be described as self-aggrandizing.

Collectively, these three individuals, among a number of others, probably influenced me through their written, or transcribed accounts. The phenomenology, as moving and sometimes sensational and disturbing as it was, was tempered by a spirit of serious inquiry in which humanness was maintained, and humility was not lost.

XIII

The other realm of experience that probably shaped my attitude in ways that would serve me (and I hope others) regarding encountering strange experiences, and their attendant realities, stems from a course that I took, many years ago, as a part of my doctoral work. It was a course entitled "Qualitative Research Methods."

As previously mentioned, the "scientific method" (the official ritual of scientific inquiry within the secular religion Scientism) holds that one starts with a hypothesis, which must be testable by controlled experiments, producing, to be valid, replicable results. If the hypothesis tests out, and subsequent experiments replicate the findings, there is a statistical basis on which to pin a result—a finding—and the result becomes a component of a theory, which in turn will generate additional testable hypotheses, and so on. Such is the march of scientific progress, which relies generally on quantifiable results — on statistically based inquiry, analysis and reporting. This is quantitative research. It is a powerful method.

*Qual*itative research, as I was to learn, is equally as "rigorous" as its anointed quantitative cousin, but its basis is entirely different.

In qualitative research and analysis, one starts with neither theory nor hypothesis. The challenge within qualitative research is, in the absence of theory and hypothesis, to immerse oneself in an environment as participant-observer, have direct encounter with whatever is going on around one, keep copious field notes of one's observations, and then, as a final act, see if the field notes start to subdivide into subsuming categories, yielding data that would be suggestive of hypotheses that can then be further explored.

I well recall one of our first qualitative research course field assignments. We were directed to go into a bar as if we were aliens visiting from another world, without any prior orientation or bias regarding humankind and human earthly existence.[10] We were to observe, and record field notes, as if our perspective — our experiential background — were completely *other* than human.

While writing this commentary, I actually (after all these years!) came up with my field notes from this assignment. Here are some excerpts from them:

Verbal transcript of field notes — delayed recall

Site: Applebee's, Newton, MA

---

10) Indeed, one of the classic texts in the field of qualitative research is a published study called *The Cocktail Waitress* (see bibliography).

Site visit: 2/23/88   Recall: 2/26 and 2/29, 1988.

Walking into dimly lit enclosure. Thumpa, thumpa, thumpa. Layout: barrier with flat counter surface, arranged as a square in center of chamber. Illumination in chamber is low. Small clusters of murmuring, huddling life-forms. Two female life forms ambulate from cluster to cluster. One of these female life-forms is tall, thin and tight-lipped. Other is tall, fuller and slinky, with form-fitting outerwear, bright red. This female life form appears to be engaging in hypnosis or rhythmic entrainment exercises with male life forms, as deportment of the latter appears to alter markedly when in the presence of this female life form. Catch sight of her two appendages clasping small greenish object, appearing to rasp or wring same with minor appendages which extend from major ones. Fluid substance flows out which female lets gravitational field influence to enter clear cylinder positioned below. Female form also is in receipt of additional cylinders containing viscous material. Oval crystalline forms (as viewed from top), cylindrical (as viewed from side)—open at one end (retainer at other end). Within open-ended crystalline cylinders are cube forms—also crystalline (somewhat grainy) emitting colder local atmosphere. Cold cube forms are partially (mostly) enveloped in non-solid, flowing, permeable, semi-clear material. Other life-forms (both male and female) have similar cylinders—elevate via appendages to central entrance pore of organism, upend cylinders, and take in flowing matter. Male life form approaches area where three of us observers are huddled. Strange that male life form visits us! Usually excursions outside of square barrier arrangement are undertaken by female life-forms, and this male entity remains inside/within square barrier. Feeling is that we must let this male entity bring us something so that we can fit in to milieu. Otherwise our cover as observers will be blown. "Would you like anything?" Verbal form with inflection suggests inter-rogatory interaction. I specify assent for an arrangement of representational forms in the following sequence

G-I-N-G-E-R-A-L-E. We get past this exercise. From top of chamber, at adjacent corners, are two enclosures. Frontal area of each enclosure features moving images of indigenous life-forms in a colored, yet phosphorous-tinged type of illumination. Life-forms, though huddled near one another, may be turning their attention to different phosphorous screens, thereby appearing indifferent to one another even though they are in close proximity to each other. Life-forms in chamber either are in partially reclined attitude, surrounding elevated, flat surfaces distributed fairly evenly throughout chamber, or are positioned on more highly elevated small discs, running along the periphery of the square, flat-topped barrier. Each small, elevated disc is supported by four circular struts. At one end of square barrier (at right angle) is a box with rows of pressure points, each of which has engraved symbols on it. Several rows consist of one color of pressure points, while adjoining rows have other colors of pressure points. The female inserts flexible rectangular cards into box with pressure points and applies pressure to various sequences of these pressure points.

Whew! What a challenge it was (an impossible one, of course) to attempt to remove the biases of human conditioning and culturally determined points of reference from our observations. Yet the challenge to aspire to "neutral status" as an observer remains a worthy goal, nonetheless.

However, the bigger lesson of *applied* qualitative research is this: *Wherever* one finds oneself, one can engage in field research and, as participant-observer, take note of, and generate theory about, that in which one is immersed. Unlike the quantitative research of consensus science, in which areas of potential inquiry are dismissed either because they don't lend themselves to quantitative analysis or because they are otherwise deemed unworthy of study, qualitative research methodology dismisses no area of inquiry out of hand on the grounds of being necessarily unworthy, or stymyingly inaccessible. There are *always* experiences or environments in which to become immersed, fresh observations to be noted with a developed, discerning consciousness, and fresh theory to be inferred from grounded observations.

This way of going about research is actually nothing new to any of us. From the vantage point of making sense of our lives, we are, each and every one of us, engaged in qualitative research and analysis whether we want to be or not. Each of us has an existence sourced in mystery. We parachute in, so to speak, to an utterly foreign, four-dimensional space-time existence — in other words, we are birthed into history — and we make sense of, and develop our own orientation around, who we are and what we are doing here entirely on the basis of our grounded existence in this reality, as shaped and buffeted by the forces of genetic inheritance, family history and parenting, ethnicity, schooling, religion, the law, society-at-large, and so on, as mediated and shaped by our interactively developing neurology.

One of our many acquisitions, as we develop a "theory of ourselves" (a.k.a. our "identity") involves the notion of our being a separate, detached observer capable of suspending our participatory presence long enough to assume a neutrality — a dispassionate, uninvolved, unaffected-by, at-a-remove, objectivity — regarding that which we observe. Along the way, we may come to subscribe to the scientific method as holding the keys to ultimate revelation and truth. However, our acquisition of *that* viewpoint is an overlay — a later arrival to the basic qualitative reality and sense-making that surrounds us — that impinges upon us and perfuses us from all directions. Extracting a sense of objectivity from the ground of the subjective is a process that we have already been engaged with, and will be engaging in, at every point along the time-line of our lives. Lamentably, for those who need to preserve a fragile sanity and sense of the primacy of egoistic individuality, the apparent validity of being able to function from a perspective of detached objectivity, along with the notion that this standard constitutes the sine qua non for determining what is factually "real" or "true," are questionable assumptions at best, and fanciful delusions at worst. For better or worse, any "assumption," any "taking for granted," that we *ever* (with or without forethought) adopt, a priori, as a starting point, for our more rigorous, rational "scientific" inquiries, deliberations and formulations have their rootedness in the opaqueness of subjective reality. Whether acknowledged or not, at the root of any "knowing" is *always* immersion in the subjective. There can be nothing known without a knower, with all of his/her individual particularities and predispositions, construing something in a manner that is perceived as *knowing* it. There can be no "objective" fact pried loose without the evaluative interaction — the participation-in-relation-with — of the scrutinizer. This state of affairs — this grounding of the rational, discursive, observing, "distanced" faculty in the subjective — *is* the inescapable reality.

Our individual lives, and the *individuality* within them, do not lend themselves at all well to experiments of a quantitative nature. *Populations* of individuals can be studied and made to yield statistically significant findings. However, the questions we can fathom through a study of populations are not the personal ones that matter most: Who am I? Where did I come from? Why am I here? Where am I going? What is the meaning of my life? Why is there *anything*?

Quantitative research and consensus science undoubtedly have contributions to make to these questions of ultimate concern. Indeed, the contributions of science are beyond question — as are its perils. However, quantitative methods are unlikely to yield ultimate answers. Qualitative research may fare no better — but at least it does not flinch from encountering random or quirky, highly personal (and perhaps highly relevant) experience and phenomenology, whatever they may be — and it accepts, and emboldens, a sense-making born of acknowledged, participatory consciousness on the part of the experiencer.

So . . . although my exposure to Monroe, Streiber, Cayce (and many others) and a qualitative research methods course in graduate school all took place two and a half decades ago (plus or minus), in regarding the extraordinary and moving experiences that constituted the fruition of my loving relationship with my dear friend Wilbur, I suppose that the biases, or tendencies, to honor phenomenology on its own terms, and to *stay with it* (the phenomenology), regardless of the ineluctable muddle of subjectivity that this entails, and to try to forgo either rejecting the whole enterprise as "unworthy" of study, on the one hand, or going the way of constructing yet another metaphysic, on the other, were somehow engendered in me via these earlier exposures.

All of the above, then, constitutes *my* bias — how I observe things, how I came by this way of sense-making, and so on.

Those thoroughly indoctrinated in the tenets of Scientisim will find what I have presented above easy to dismiss. Yet hopefully, some may feel more emboldened to explore the possibilities of exercising discriminating observation in areas not readily quantifiable, and come to recognize the value in doing so.

The truly need-bound religious may feel a pang of disappointment that that which I have to offer by way of shedding light on the question of the continuation of consciousness post-bodily-death presents this likelihood in a rather paltry—and rational, rather than "faith-based"—manner, as more a component of generic human consciousness, *regardless* of the presence or absence of any particular creed, theistic tether or specific observance or devotion. To them I would say that maybe it's time to broaden your views of what being of human kind truly entails.

To those who feel, whether conscientiously or smugly, among the elect due to scrupulous religious observance, the tenets of a dogma, or claimed spiritual attainment—if this account strikes you as holding the possibility of having actually transpired—of being true—I hope that you can loosen your grip a bit on the strictures of your faith to ponder what experiences befell a confirmed atheist and someone whose own spiritual life probably more strongly resembles heathenism than any of the "creeds."

And for those of you among the heathen or dispossessed who feel no connection to yourself as a mystery, perhaps the narrative, along with this qualitatively-derived commentary and analysis, can embolden you to be more open to direct encounters of all sorts—including the plane of uncomplicated loving friendship, and to *dare* to experience what is there. You never know what is 'round the next bend. You never know what (or who) may await. You never know when, or if, the Universe may suddenly convulse into yet another flip of the cat's cradle and reveal a facet of Itself to you—of *you* to you—you never knew existed.

On this hopeful, adventurous note I bid you well. My wish for you?

— *Dare* to stay tuned . . .

I believe that Wilbur would wish as much for you, as well.

Epilogue

Wilbur with friend (of whom he had many)

The Winter of 2004–05

It is now March, 2005, about six weeks shy of the fourth anniversary of Wilbur's death. This winter has been strange, and hopefully only an aberration from the norm—although I suspect something more far-reaching is taking hold. For the first time in the thirty-seven winters I have skated the Sudbury, *there was no skating on the river this winter.*

An early snow and some cold arrived in late November/early December, then tepid temperatures—no ice—prevailed all through December on into the second week of January. A lengthy, vintage cold snap then hit, but it was accompanied by very windy conditions, which stymied the formation of a smooth, thick layer of black ice, and before such a base of ice could become firmly established, a major snowstorm hit, dumping around two feet of snow. With all that snow overlaying a very iffy foundation of ice, it was not safe to venture on the river by foot, and, of course, skating was impossible.

What was needed was a good January thaw, which could melt that ice/snow sandwich down to a flat, liquid-puddled surface, and then another hard freeze, as in "River ice, take two!" This kind of sequence, in a typical winter, might occur once, perhaps two times. What actually happened this winter was . . . weird. There was *no* January thaw. The nut-cracking freeze persisted into late January, keeping the unsafe ice-snow sandwich congealed. Without a "second take," it could not be safe, let alone skatable.

A thaw finally hit in early February, creating some open water—welcome under the circumstances. By this point, I knew that the odds were already growing long that there would be any skatable ice. In those thirty-seven winters on the Sudbury, I had only noted one winter, many years earlier, in which, with open water in dominance by February 1st, the Sudbury had refrozen sufficiently to bring forth extended river skating.

But as it turned out, no real freeze happened in February. The one remaining cold snap of the winter happened . . . in early March! It combined with a trifecta of late-winter snows, somewhat anomalous. Most river water remained open. Even more peculiar, during this winter's last-gasp cold blast the Charles River basin between Boston and Cambridge actually covered over with a surreal layer of sludge soup that extended all the way down to the Charles River Canal by the Museum of Science—sweet to look at, but oh, so treacherous! While this congealed "glurp" was clogging the lower Charles, the upper Charles, in Watertown, remained open water—the absolute inverse of how a "freeze" usually transpires on the Charles. Go figure: How weird is that?! (There were even crew boats, with their oarsmen and women, out plying the frigid waters of the upper Charles even while the lower basis [between MIT in Cambridge and the Back Bay in Boston] was still "glurped over.")

In summary, notwithstanding the variation and range in the timing and extent of cycles of freeze and thaw in any given winter, the complete closing out of skating during this winter of 2004–05 is an anomaly of such note that I can only attribute it to the persistent northerly embrace of global warming.

This makes me wonder . . . Thirty-seven winters from now, will the presence of skatable ice on the Sudbury become as rare an event as, looking back, the winter of 2004–05 has been as a *non*-skating event?

Will the magic that sparked that wonderful relationship with Wilbur turn out to have been a specific, non-recurring event — not because Wilbur has died and because one day I will be gone, but because the setting — river ice in Eastern Massachusetts — will have faded beyond rarity into nonexistence?

CONCERNING WILBUR'S POST-DEATH VISIT

There have been no subsequent visitations by Wilbur that I'm aware of — *and* I have *not* become some New Age crackpot claiming to be in regular communion with spirits. Nor am I (last I checked) listed on any registry as a visionary or mystic. It's not necessarily that I have been unreceptive to the possibility of a follow-up visit. I love Wilbur and I would love to see him again — in whatever form. However, I find a certain charm in the fact that his visit was, apparently, a "one-off."

Somehow, the subjective — experiential — truth (to me) that a post-death visit actually occurred seems bolstered by the fact that it "only happened once." It supports my speculation that whatever energy constituted "Wilbur," post-death, made the effort to "cross the divide" to reach me, as yet embodied, for the purpose of honoring the obligation Wilbur knowingly took on prior to his death. Having honored such an obligation, he made his point; there was no need to gild the lily. Wilbur would never have countenanced such a redundant expenditure of energy.

It's odd. My life goes on, and I don't find that I'm particularly preoccupied with having been so visited. However, every once in a while—often while lying in bed late at night, awake—it will hit me that this thing happened to me—that such an effort was mobilized, from "the other side," to reach me, and that this effort was successful—not only successful in terms of having reached me, but successful as well in that "the other side" "knew" that it had been successful in getting through to me and, in that priceless moment, was also able to receive my own acknowledgement and loving response to what was happening. When such thoughts arise, I can feel a smile of contentment spread across my face. I just continue to feel so enriched by having had such an experience. The experience continues to abide in me as a reality that is self-evident and, in an utterly indescribable way, ever present.

Not so long ago a former psychotherapy client of mine was diagnosed with terminal cancer. She had written a moving account of her therapy and her post-therapy years and, once she knew her diagnosis to be terminal, she contacted me to enlist my assistance in editing and publishing her book. Initially, I did not leap at the opportunity, but, as it became increasingly clear that her time was growing short and she needed to have the burden of her book's destiny lifted from her, I assented. As the legal work got done, and the formalities of copyright transfer and royalty arrangements were finalized, I could tell that my former client still had some anxiety and uncertainty about what would become of her work.

Matter of factly, I just told her that, after she had died, should she have the awareness of being dissatisfied, for any reason, with the arrangements we had agreed to regarding her book, if she were to "come to visit me in my dream life" and express her reservations, I would immediately dissolve our agreement, and the book would revert back to the custody and safe-keeping of her estate.

I had earlier mentioned the "Wilbur" visit to her (without perseverating on it), so she knew that I was serious in presenting this option to her, and assuring her that it exists. This "guarantee" of mine served to lay her anxiety to rest, completely.

This experience with my former client bears witness to the longer-term effects Wilbur's visit has had on me. I experience my life as existing in a context in which it seems "obvious," and "matter of fact," to me, that such arrangements are possible.

VIVIAN

Now entering her mid-eighties, Vivian is as committed as ever to packing a lot into the stream of life. She was an honored guest at Emily's and my wedding in June, 2003. She is currently reading Thucydides on the Peloponnesian Wars as part of a course she is taking at Harvard; over this past winter she had her kitchen redone for the first time in over forty years, and she has recently been interviewed for an article on stereo-imaging technology, about which she is considered an expert.

I shared with her, with baited breath, a copy of the first draft of the manuscript for this book. I didn't know how she would take it, as she is staunch in her ways as a trained scientist, and not given to any New Age coddling.

I delivered a copy of the manuscript to her in August, 2004 at her (and Wilbur's) old place on Cape Breton. Much to my surprise, she vetted the manuscript with alacrity. She was very helpful with correcting certain inaccuracies around dates and other historical circumstances, and did not disown me on the matter of "visitation." Her opening comment, as a prelude to several pages of carefully considered, handwritten notes was, "Steve, the manuscript is impressive." I am grateful to have such a wonderful, tolerant friend.

Curiously, my older daughter moved back into the area a few years ago, in the midst of a transition that was not unfolding too smoothly for her. She lived with Vivian for about a year, taking sanctuary in the same second-floor room where I had, a number of years earlier, shaken, rattled and rolled my way through my own mid-life demolition. Her experience living with Vivian in that Conantum neighborhood home was as healing for her, in its own way, as it had been for me.

Vivian and I have visited periodically, usually coinciding with my driving east from Western Massachusetts towards Boston late on a Wednesday evening. She is still a night owl, so the lateness of the visiting hour, as I come through Concord, seems to be to her liking.

As she has gradually been going through Wilbur's things, she has enlisted my assistance on a couple of occasions regarding the disposition of Wilbur's old collection of vacuum tubes and associated vacuum tube-era "glow-bug" electronics. She gave me a beautiful, vintage (1953), RME-4350 ham radio receiver of his, and this receiver now occupies an honored place in the "AM" (Amplitude Modulation—often called, nowadays, "ancient modulation" by the current crop of ham radio techno-snobs) operating post at amateur radio station K1REX. It is a joy to use.

On another occasion Vivian offered me the opportunity to go through several pairs of ice skates and take what I thought I could use. My feet are quite a bit larger than Wilbur's; however, I had a hunch that the skates he used towards the end of his life, a beautiful pair of Bauer hockey skates, would not go to waste. I was right. They just happened to fit my younger daughter's feet perfectly. She aspires to move like winged Mercury when she wears them. Those skates, in use, strike me as a suitable living memorial to Wilbur. I think he would be pleased.

Vivian took keen notice of how there was not skatable ice on the Sudbury this past winter (2004 –2005). We've commiserated on this. Neither of us was tempted to set foot on the river all winter long.

AFTERTHOUGHTS ON "PATHWAYS"

In the "Commentary & Analysis" section, I brought up the notion of how a person is "reachable" by energies and initiatives from "the other side." I presented, both in the text and the commentary, something of how my own pathways had developed — or, more likely, had been developed.

The additional insight that comes to me about this is that if we (conceptually) subdivide our bodies into ever smaller components and units of constituent elements, we extend (with our mind's eye) through organ systems, muscular-skeletal, circulatory and respiratory systems (among numerous others), neurological networks, tissues, individual cells, molecules, atomic structure and so on, reaching ever more microscopically into the subatomic, or quantum realm. At the quantum level those constituents that comprise us obey quantum laws of probability—the world of quantum mechanics. This is also the scale assayed by string theory—increasingly positing the underlying "stuff" that comprises us as *not* stuff at all, but rather nodal points of vibrational resonance.

At this level of energy, our beings are connected to—enmeshed in—through the uncanny phenomenology of the quantum world, the "all that is" in ways that stand time and space on their respective ears (as rigorously affirmed by quantum-level experiments). These "edges" of our being, which impinge on us from every "direction" and in every "moment," I am increasingly persuaded, are in constant correspondence with this "larger"—more extensive—reality that creates and supports us, including the realities of other dimensions, the existence of which is inferred from the mathematics of string theory.

Having a concept of this quantum-level interpenetration—even if this concept is not literally correct—is like finding permission to (be) "open" to encountering new ranges of experience. A "concept," in this sense, is a kind of mental map—an inferred reality—that precedes the discovery of what "terrain" is actually there to be mapped out and explored. Such a concept may also precede awakening to what ranges of reality may be "in waiting"—waiting for *their* opportunity to discover and explore *us*.

Framing a concept—reflecting on the further reaches of human nature—can then embolden us to open to an encounter with such possibilities. I feel drawn to this, as I once felt drawn to a frozen river in the dead of winter—there to discover the "life" that abounds, a portion of which was "Wilbur."

Today, when there *is* ice (as I hope there will be again), I have now become, and am, that "strange, white-haired man" out there on those beautiful reaches, ever beckoning further exploration—as punctuated by wonderful, sometimes quirky, chance meetings with those who also are beginning to heed the call to venture out upon river ice, offering, with as much love and care as I can summon, words of greeting, enthusiasm, caution, instruction, and joy.

Selected Readings

Benson, Herbert, M.D. *The Relaxation Response*. New York: Avon, 1976.

Boa, Fraser. *The Way of the Dream: Conversations on Jungian Dream Interpretation with Marie-Louise von Franz*. Boston: Shambhala, 1994.

Boznak, Robert. *A Little Course in Dreams*. Boston, Shambhala, 1986.

Committee for the Scientific Investigation of Claims of the Paranormal (CSICOP). *Skeptical Inquirer*. Periodical published bimonthly. (CSICOP, Box 703, Amherst, New York 14226— http://www.csicop.org/si/).

Fox, Mark. *Religion, Spirituality and the Near-Death Experience*. New York: Routledge, 2003.

Harner, Michael. *The Way of the Shaman*. New York: Harper and Row, 1990.

Ingerman, Sandra. *Soul Retrieval: Mending the Fragmented Self through Shamanic Practice*. New York: HarperSanFrancisco, 1991.

King, Serge Kahili. *Earth Energies: A Quest for the Hidden Power of the Planet*. Wheaton, Illinois: Quest Books, 1992.

Kübler-Ross, Elisabeth. *On Life After Death*. Berkeley, California: Celestial Arts, 1991.

Laberge, Stephen. *Lucid Dreaming*. Los Angeles: Jeremy P. Tarcher, 1985.

Maslow, Abraham H. *Toward a Psychology of Being*. Princeton, New Jersey: D. Van Nostrand Company, 1962.

Moody, Raymond, M.D. *Life after Life: The Investigation of a Phenomenon—Survival of Bodily Death*. New York: Bantam, 1976.

_____. *Reunions: Visionary Encounters with Departed Loved Ones*. New York: Villard, 1993.

Munroe, Robert A. *Journeys Out of the Body*. New York: Doubleday, 1971.

_____. *Far Journeys*. New York: Doubleday, 1985.

Spradley, James P. *The Cocktail Waitress: Women's Work in a Man's World*. New York: McGraw-Hill, 1975.

Stearns, Jess. *Edgar Cayce: The Sleeping Prophet*. New York: Bantam, 1968.

Strieber, Whitley. *Communion: A True Story*. New York: Beechtree Books, 1987.

_____. *Transformation: The Breakthrough*. New York: Beechtree Books, 1988.

van der Post, Laurens. *Jung and the Story of Our Time*. New York: Pantheon, 1975.

You-know-who, "shooting the duck" (while going back-wards!) on black ice on the Sudbury (winter of 2007) at the ripe old age of 60. I got "all the way down," and "all the way back up"—ouch! (This may be the last "shoot-the-duck" my body ever lets me get away with doing—at least in this life-time.)

ABOUT THE AUTHOR

Stephen Rich Merriman has skated the Sudbury River in Eastern Massachusetts for forty winters. He lives in San Francisco, where he works as a corporate consultant, psychotherapist and jazz pianist. He enjoys his professional life roles. He enjoys even more the personal ones: those of husband, father and grandfather. Each January he packs his skates and heads back to the Sudbury in search of some ice. So far, so good.

Printed in the United States
154301LV00001B/12/P

9 780981 769813